FRIENDSHIP'S GARLAND

FRIENDSHIP'S GARLAND

BEING THE

CONVERSATIONS, LETTERS, AND OPINIONS
OF THE LATE

ARMINIUS

BARON VON THUNDER-TEN-TRONCKH

COLLECTED AND EDITED

WITH A DEDICATORY LETTER TO ADOLESCENS LEO, ESQ.

OF "THE DAILY TELEGRAPH"

BY

MATTHEW ARNOLD

GYAN

Published by

Gyan Publishing House
5, Ansari Road
Daryaganj, New Delhi-110002
Phone: 011-47034999, 9811692060
E-mail: books@gyanbooks.com

Distribution Network
gyanbooks.com
India, USA, Canada, UK, Australia, France

ISBN : 978-81-212-2558-8 (HB)
First Published, 1903

2nd Impression 2021

Printed at: Gyan Press, Delhi.

Friendship's Garland
Author: Matthew Arnold

FRIENDSHIP'S GARLAND

BEING THE

CONVERSATIONS, LETTERS, AND OPINIONS

OF THE LATE

ARMINIUS
BARON VON THUNDER-TEN-TRONCKH

COLLECTED AND EDITED

WITH A DEDICATORY LETTER TO ADOLESCENS LEO, Esq.

OF "THE DAILY TELEGRAPH"

BY MATTHEW ARNOLD

. . . *manibus date lilia plenis*

POPULAR EDITION.

LONDON

JOHN MURRAY, ALBEMARLE STREET, W.

1903

CONTENTS.

DEDICATORY LETTER.

My dear Leo,— *Grub Street, Candlemas Day,* 1871.

Shall I ever forget the evening, at the end of last November, when your feeling letter describing the death of our friend first met my eyes? I was alone in my garret; it was just dark; my landlady opened the door and threw a paper on the table. Selfish creatures that we are! my first thought was: It is a communication from the Literary Fund! The straits to which I am reduced by my long warfare with the Philistines, have at last, I said to myself, become known; they have excited sympathy; this is no doubt a letter from Mr. Octavian Blewitt, enclosing half-a-crown, the promise of my dinner at Christmas, and the kind wishes of Lord Stanhope for my better success in authorship. Hastily I lighted my lamp, and saw the *Pall Mall Gazette.* You know, Leo, how, after vainly knocking at the door of the *Daily Telegraph,* I carried to Northumberland Street my records of the conversations of Arminius. I love to think that the success of the 'Workhouse Casual' had disposed the Editor's heart to be friendly towards Pariahs; my communication was affably accepted, and from that day to this the *Pall Mall Gazette*, whenever there is any mention in it of Arminius, reaches me in Grub Street *gratis*. I took the paper, I opened it; your playful signature caught my eye. I read your letter through to the end, and then . . . .

Suffer me, Leo, to draw a veil over those first days of grief. In the tumult of feeling plans were then formed to which I have not energy to give effect. I nourished the design of laying before the public a complete account of Arminius von Thunder-ten-Tronckh, and of the group which was gathered round him. The history of his family has been written by the famous Voltaire in his *Candide*; but I doubt whether an honest man can in conscience send the British public to even the historical works of that dangerous author. Yet a singular fortune brought together in our set the descendants of a number of the personages of *Candide*. Von Thunder-ten-Tronckh is, perhaps, sufficiently made known by the following letters; his curious delusion about the living representative of Pangloss is also fully noticed there. But not a glimpse, alas, do these records give of our poor friend Martin (de Mabille), who has just been shut up in Paris eating rats, the cynical descendant of that great foe of Pangloss's optimism, the Martin of *Candide*. Hardly a glimpse is given of the Marquis Pompeo Pococurante, little Pompey with the soft eyes and dark hair, whose acquaintance you made at Turin under the *portiques du Pô*, and whom you brought to London in the hope of curing, by the spectacle of the *Daily Telegraph*, his hereditary indifference and ennui. Of our English friends, too, the public would, doubtless, be glad to hear more. Mr. Bottles himself fills, in the following letters, by no means that space to which his importance entitles him; the excellent Baptist minister, for whom Mr. Bottles has so high a regard, the Rev. Josiah Jupp, appears far too unfrequently; your *Mary Jane*, Leo, is a name and nothing more; hardly more than names are my good and kind patroness, the late lamented Mrs. Bottles, and her sister and successor, Miss Hannah. It is a small matter, perhaps; but I should have liked, too, the public to know something of my faithful landlady here in Grub Street, Kitty Crone, on whom, after my vain conflict with the Philistines is ended, will probably devolve the pious duty of closing my eyes.

I had imagined a memorial of Arminius, in which all these would have found their place; but my spirits broke down in the attempt to execute my design. All, therefore, that I have done is to collect the stray records of Arminius which have already been published, to illustrate them with notes so far as appeared necessary, and to give myself the melancholy pleasure of dedicating to you, Leo, a collection which owes to your brilliant and facile pen some of its best ornaments.

Our friend had an odd way of showing it, but certainly Arminius had a love for this country. Do you remember, Leo, that conversation in the summer of last year, the last we spent together in his company? It was in the arbour of the garden of the 'Bald-Faced Stag' at Finchley. We had all been to the gallery of the House of Commons to hear Mr. Vernon Harcourt develop a system of unsectarian religion from the Life of Mr. Pickwick; but from some obstacle or other the expected treat did not come off. We adjourned to Finchley, and there, you remember, Arminius began with a discourse on religious education. He exacted from me, as you know, the promise not, as he harshly phrased it, to 'make a hash of his ideas' by reporting them to the public; and the promises of friendship are sacred. But afterwards the conversation became general. It then took a wider range; and I remember Mr. Frederic Harrison beginning to harangue, with his usual fiery eloquence, on the enervation of England, and on the malignancy of all the brute mass of us who are not

Comtists. Arminius checked him. 'Enervation!'—said he; 'depend upon it, yours is still the most fighting people in the whole world. Malignancy!—the best character of the English people ever yet given, friendly as the character is, is still this of Burke's: "The ancient and inbred integrity, piety, good nature, and good humour of the people of England." Your nation is sound enough, if only it can be taught that being able to do what one likes, and say what one likes, is not sufficient for salvation. Its dangers are from a surfeit of clap-trap, due to the false notion that liberty and publicity are not only valuable for the use to be made of them, but are goods in themselves, nay, are the *summum bonum*!'

To the same effect he wrote to me from before Paris, a week or two before his death. 'You know I do not join in the common dislike of your nation, or in the belief in its certain decay. But no nation can, without danger, go on stuffing its mind with such nonsense as is talked by the newspapers which you are stupid (*sic*) enough to quote with admiration. "The Germans, forsooth," says your precious *Telegraph*, "cannot too soon begin the lesson, of which England has been the special teacher, that national greatness and wealth are to be prized only in so far as they ensure the freedom of the individual citizen, and the right of all to join in free debate. Without that liberty, a

German Empire will be only a gilded despotism, politically weak in spite of its military power, barbaric in spite of its schools and universities." "The fall," says your *Daily News*, "of the late Government of France is history's re-assertion of the principle of political liberty." Do you not see that, if France, without political liberty, has signally lost, and Germany, without political liberty, has signally won, it is absurd to make the presence or absence of political liberty in themselves the ground of the fall or success of nations? Of the fall or success of nations, certain *virtues* are the ground; political, ay, and social liberty, are, if you like, favourable to those virtues, where a root of them already exists; therefore I am a Republican;—but they by no means ensure them. If you have not these virtues, and imagine that your political liberty will pull you through without them, you will be ruined in spite of your political liberty. I admire England because she has such a root in her of these virtues; not because they have given her, among other good things, political liberty. Your fetish-worship of mere liberty is, on the contrary, just now the gravest danger to you. Your newspapers are every day solemnly saying that the great lesson to be learned from the present war is so and so,—always something which it is not. There are many lessons to be learned from the present war; I will tell you what is for *you* the great lesson to be learned from it:—*obedience.* That, instead of every man airing his self-consequence, thinking it bliss to talk at random about things, and to put his finger in every pie, you should seriously understand that there is a *right* way of doing things, and that the bliss is, without thinking of one's self-consequence, to do them in that way, or to forward their being done,—this is the great lesson your British public, as you call it, has to learn, and may learn, in some degree, from the Germans in this war! Englishmen were once famous for the power of holding their tongues and doing their business, and, therefore, I admire your nation. The business now to be done in the world is harder than ever, and needs far more than has been ever yet needed of thought, study, and seriousness; miscarry you must, if you let your daily doses of clap-trap make you imagine that liberty and publicity can be any substitute for these.'

I doubt whether this is sound, Leo, and, at any rate, the *D. T.* should have been more respectfully mentioned; but it shows that the feeling of Arminius towards this country was at bottom tender. My own patriotism, as you know, never wavered, even while I made myself, in a manner, the mouthpiece of Arminius, and submitted to the predominance which his intellect, I own, exercised over me. My affection for him remains as strong as ever, but now that his life is ended, and his predominance withdrawn, I feel that a new destiny is probably opening for me. My patriotic feelings will henceforth have free play; the iron hand of Arminius will no longer press them down. Your counsels, Leo, the study of our newspapers, the spectacle of our grandeur, will work with these my natural feelings; I shall earn the public approbation, I shall not be always an Ishmael. I shall ally myself to some of those great Liberal movements which,—however Arminius might choose to call them petty aimless activities, bustle without any *Ernst der ins Ganze geht*,—seem to me admirably suited to the genius of our national life, and highly productive of enjoyable excitement and honourable importance to their promoters.

We are now on the point of commencing what Arminius, with his fatally carping spirit, called our 'Thyesteän banquet of clap-trap;'—we are on the eve of the meeting of Parliament. Mr. T. Chambers will again introduce that enfranchising measure, against which I have had some prejudices, but which you, Leo, have so eloquently upheld—the bill for enabling a man to marry his deceased wife's sister. Mr. Miall, that Israelite indeed, will resume, on a more stupendous scale than ever, his labours for making all bitterness, and wrath, and anger, and clamour, and evil-speaking be put away from us, with all malice; and for our enjoyment of the pure milk of Christianity. The devoted adversaries of the Contagious Diseases Act will spread through the length and breadth of the land a salutary discussion of this equivocal measure and of all matters connected with it; and will thus, at the same time that they oppose immorality, enable the followers of even the very straitest sects of Puritanism to see life. Some of these workers will doubtless suffer me to put my hand to their plough. Like the tailor to the poet Cowper, to some one or other of them I may be allowed to make my modest appeal:—

> Say, shall *my* little bark attendant sail,
> Pursue the triumph, and partake the gale?

If not on the hustings or the platform, at least I may do something in the closet, with the pen! My mind full of this new thought, as I passed down Regent Street yesterday, and saw in a shop-window, in the frontispiece to one of Mr. Hepworth Dixon's numerous but well-merited editions, the manly and animated features of the author of the immortal *Guide to Mormonism*, I could not help exclaiming with pride: 'I, too, am an author!'

And then, Leo, comes the reaction. I look up and see Arminius's vacant stool; I sniff, and my nostrils no longer catch the scent of his tobacco. The dreams of excitement and ambition fly away; I am left solitary with the remembrance of the past, and with those consolations of piety and religion, which you, Leo, have outgrown. Yet how can I do you such an injustice?—when at this very moment my chief consolation, under our heavy bereavement, is in repeating to myself that glorious passage you read to me the other day from one of your unpublished articles for the *D. T.*:—'*In the Garden of the Hesperides, the inscrutable-eyed Sphinx whispers, with half-parted lips, Mysteries more than Eleusinian of the Happy Dead!*'

Believe me, my dear Leo,

Your faithful admirer,

MATTHEW ARNOLD.

To

ADOLESCENS LEO, ESQ.

&c. &c. &c.

(THE acquaintance of the ever-to-be-lamented Arminius was made by the present Editor on the Continent in the year 1865. The early history of the noble family of Von Thunder-ten-Tronckh, to which Arminius belonged, their establishment in Westphalia, the sack of their castle in the middle of the last century by the Bulgarians, the fate of their principal dependents (among whom was the famous optimist philosopher, Dr. Pangloss), the adventures of Arminius's grandfather and his deportation to the Jesuits at Rome, are recorded in a well-known treatise of Voltaire. Additional information is supplied in several of the following letters.

Arminius came to England in 1866, and the correspondence now given in a collected form to the public commenced in the summer of that year, at the outbreak of the war between Prussia and Austria. Many will yet remember the thrill with which they originally received, through the unworthy ministry of the present Editor, the communication of the great doctrine of 'Geist.' What, then, must it have been to hear that doctrine in its first newness from the lips of Arminius himself! Yet it will, I hope, be admitted, that even in this position of exceptional privilege, the present Editor succeeded in preserving his coolness, his independent judgment, and his proper feelings as a Briton.)—ED.

LETTER I.

I introduce Arminius and 'Geist' to the British Public.

SIR,— *Grub Street, July* 19, 1866.

A PRUSSIAN acquaintance of mine, one of the party of foreigners who so offensively criticised my countrymen to me when I was abroad last year, has been over here just now, and for the last week or so he has been favouring me with his remarks on all he hears us say about the present crisis in Germany. In confidence I will own to you that he makes himself intensely disagreeable. He has the harsh, arrogant, Prussian way of turning up his nose at things and laying down the law about them ; and though, as a lover of intellect, I admire him, and, as a seeker of truth, I value his frankness, yet, as an Englishman, and a member of what the *Daily Telegraph* calls 'the Imperial race,' I feel so uncomfortable under it, that I want, through your kindness, to call to my aid the great British public, which never loses heart and has always a bold front and a rough word ready for its assailants.

My Prussian friend got a little mortification at the beginning of his visit, and as it is my belief this mortification set him wrong from the first, I shall relate what it was. I took him with me down to Reigate by the railroad, and in the carriage was one of our representative industrial men (something in the bottle way), a famous specimen of that great middle class whose energy and self-reliance make England what it is, and who give the tone to our Parliament and to our policy. News had just come of the first bloodshed between the Austrians and Prussians now at war together in Germany. 'So they've begun fighting,' cried my countryman; 'what fools they both are!' And he handed us *Punch* with that masterly picture in it of 'Denmark avenged;' that scathing satire which represents the King of Denmark sitting with his glass of grog and his cigar, to gloat over the terrible retribution falling upon his great enemy Prussia for her misdeeds towards him. My Prussian glared at the striking moral lesson thus brought to his notice, but rage and contempt made him speechless. I hastened, with a few sentences taken from Mr. Gladstone's recent advice to the Roumanians, to pay my homage to the great principles of peaceful, industrial development which were invoked by my countryman. 'Yes; war,' I said, 'interrupts business, and brings intolerable inconvenience with it; whereas people have only to persist steadily in the manufacture of bottles, railways, banks, and finance companies, and all good things will come to them of their own accord.' Before I had finished we reached Reigate, and I got my still speechless Prussian quickly out of the train.

But never shall I forget the flood when speech came at last: 'The dolt! the dunderhead! His ignorance of the situation, his ignorance of Germany, his ignorance of what makes nations great, his ignorance of what makes life worth living, his ignorance of everything except bottles,—those infernal bottles!' I heard so much of all this that I am glad to forget it without going through it again with the British public. I only mention it to make the rudeness of expression in what follows less unaccountable.

The day before yesterday the *Daily News* published that powerful letter from Mr. Goldwin Smith, pronouncing in favour of the Prussian alliance. In great excitement I ran with it to my friend. 'At last I have got something,' I cried, 'which will please you; a declaration by one of our best writers, in one of our best newspapers, for a united Germany under Prussian headship. She and we are thereupon to combine to curb France. Wherever I go, I hear people admiring the letter and approving the idea.' A sardonic smile, such as Alexander von Humboldt used to have when he contemplated the late King of Prussia's missionary deaconesses, came over my Berliner's harsh countenance. 'Good God!' said he, 'the miracles that needle-gun is working! It is only a year ago you were threatening Prussia with France, and suggesting to that great and sagacious ruler, as you called him, the French Emperor, to take the Rhine Province from us; it is not six weeks since I saw him styled in this very newspaper, with the dignity usual in Englishmen at present, "the arbiter of Europe." He has done nothing in the meantime to injure you; he has done his best to keep well with you. How charmed he will be with his friends! But the declaration you are all so pleased at, who is it by?' 'Mr. Goldwin Smith,' I answered. 'I know him,' he said; 'a good writer, but a fanatic.' 'Oh, no, no,' said I; 'a man of genius and virtue.'

Without answering, my Berliner took the newspaper and read the letter. 'He should have served under Nelson,' he said, as he finished it; 'he hates a Frenchman as he does the devil. However, it is true that a preponderance in the world such as the French, thanks to your stupidity, were fast getting, is enough to make any human being, let alone a Frenchman, unbearable; and it is a good thing to have a great Germany in the world as well as a great France. It would be a good thing to have a great England too, if you would let us. But pray what is to unite Germany and England against France? What is to be the ground of sympathy between actual England and actual Germany?' 'You are a strong Liberal,' said I, 'so I can easily answer you. You are drawn towards England because of her liberalism, and away from the French Emperor because of his despotism.' 'Liberalism and despotism!' cried the Prussian; 'let us get beyond these forms and words. What unites and separates people now is *Geist*.'

I had not the slightest idea what he meant, and my looks told my bewilderment. 'I thought you had read Mr. Grant Duff's chapters on Germany,' said he. 'But Mr. Grant Duff knows what he writes about, so I suppose you have not. Your great Lord Palmerston used to call Germany "that country of d——d professors;" and the English public, which supposes professors to be people who know something, and hates anybody who knows anything, has always kept its mind as clear of my unfortunate country as it could. But I advise you, for the sake of the events now passing, to read Mr. Grant Duff's book. There you will find that in Berlin we oppose "Geist,"—*intelligence*, as you or the French might say,—to "Ungeist." The victory of "Geist" over "Ungeist" we think the great matter in the world. The same idea is at the bottom of democracy; the victory of reason and intelligence over blind custom and prejudice. So we German Liberals who believe in "Geist" have a sympathy with France and its governors, so far as they are believers in democracy. We have no sympathy with English liberalism, whose centre is in the "Ungeist" of such people as your wiseacre in the Reigate train.'

'But then you play,' cried I, 'the game of the Tories; for listen to Mr. Goldwin Smith: "The Tories in Europe, with the sure instinct of a party, recognise the great patron of reaction in the Emperor of the French." You and we are to unite, in order to defeat the Tories and the Emperor of the French.'

The Prussian answered: 'Mr. Goldwin Smith blinds himself with the passions, as the Emperor of the French himself would say, of another age. The Tories of Europe have no real love for the Emperor of the French; they may admire and envy his absolutism and strength, but they hate his fundamental principles: they can have no real sympathy with the Sovereign who says boldly that he detests the actual public law of Europe, and who tells the people that it is among the people he finds the true genius of France, and breathes freely. Such a man works for "Geist" in his way;[1] not, perhaps, through a *Daily*

[1] The indulgence of Arminius for this execrable and unsuccessful

Telegraph, or monster meetings in Trafalgar Square, or a Coles's Truss Manufactory standing where it ought not, a glorious monument of individualism and industrialism, to adorn the "finest site in Europe;" but by making the common people feel they are alive and have a human spirit in them. We North-Germans have worked for "Geist" in our way, by loving knowledge, by having the best-educated middle and lower class in the world. You see what this has just done for us. France has "Geist" in her democracy, and Prussia in her education. Where have you got it?—got it as a force, I mean, and not only in a few scattered individuals. Your common people is barbarous; in your middle class "Ungeist" is rampant; and as for your aristocracy, you know "Geist" is forbidden by nature to flourish in an aristocracy.

'So do not,' he continued, 'suffer yourself to be deceived by parallels drawn from times before "Geist." What has won this Austrian battle for Prussia is "Geist;' "Geist" has used the King, and Bismarck, and the Junkers, and "Ungeist in uniform," all for its own ends; and "Geist" will continue so to use them till it has triumphed.[1]

tyrant was unworthy of a member of our great Teutonic family. Probably, after Sedan, he changed his opinion of him.—ED.

[1] I am unwilling to triumph over Arminius in his grave; but I cannot help remarking that 'Ungeist in uniform,' as Mr. Bottles observes to me, has just given a pretty good account of the 'Geist' in

It will ally itself with "Geist" where it finds it, because there it has a ground for mutual respect and understanding; and where there is no "Geist," it has none.

'And now,' this odious man went on, 'now, my dear friend, I shall soon be leaving you, so one word more. You have lately been writing about the Celts and the Germans, and in the course of your remarks on the Germans you have said, among many impertinences, one thing which is true. You have said that the strength of North Germany lay in this, that the idea of science governed every department of human activity there. You, my dear friend, live in a country where at present the idea of clap-trap governs every department of human activity. Great events are happening in the world, and Mr. Goldwin Smith tells you that "England will be compelled to speak at last." It would be truly sad if, when she does speak, she should talk nonsense. To prevent such a disaster, I will give you this piece of advice, with which I take my leave: "*Get Geist.*"'

Thank God, this d——d professor (to speak as Lord Palmerston) is now gone back to his own *Intelligenz-Staat.*

French democracy; and I have a shrewd suspicion it will give an equally good account of the 'Geist' of Arminius's educated and liberal friends in Prussia. Perhaps Arminius was taken away from the evil to come!—ED.

I half hope there may next come a smashing defeat of the Prussians before Vienna, and make my ghostly friend laugh on the wrong side of his mouth. Meanwhile, I shall take care that he hears whatever answers he gets. I know that they will be conclusive, and I hope that they will be speedy, and in this hope,

I am, Sir,

Your obedient servant,

MATTHEW ARNOLD.

To

The EDITOR *of the* PALL MALL GAZETTE.

LETTER II.

Arminius appears as his own Interpreter.

SIR,— *Berlin, July* 31, 1866.

AN English friend of mine, Mr. Matthew Arnold, seems to have rushed into print with an idea or two he picked up from me when I was in England, and to have made rather a mess of it; at least, he sends me some newspapers which have answered him, and writes me a helpless sort of a letter at the same time, asking me how he is to parry this, and what he is to say in reply to that. Now, I have a regard for this Mr. Matthew Arnold, but I have taken his measure, and know him to be, as a disputant, rather a poor creature. Again and again I have seen him anxiously ruminating over what his adversary has happened to say against his ideas; and when I tell him (if the ideas were mine) that his adversary is a *dummkopf*, and that he must stand up to him firm and square, he begins to smile, and tells me that what is probably passing through his adversary's mind is so and so.[1]

[1] A very ill-natured and exaggerated description of my (I hope not unamiable candour.—ED.

I see your hideous truss manufactory in Trafalgar Square comes up in this controversy, and that very manufactory brings to my mind a ridiculous instance of my poor friend's weakness. I had been running over with him a few of the principal violations of æsthetic laws in London, illustrating the lesson by reference to the stucco palaces of my beautiful Berlin. After despatching the Duke of Wellington's statue and the black dome and grey pepper-boxes of your National Gallery, I came to Coles's manufactory. 'Can anything be more atrocious?' I asked. 'It is bad,' answered my poor friend; 'and yet,' he went on, 'and yet, Arminius, I have a tenderness for that manufactory. That manufactory, with other things in London like it, is one of my favourite arguments for the immortality of the soul.' 'What folly have you got in your head now?' said I. 'Remember,' said he, 'what is told us of the statue of the Olympian Zeus by Phidias. It was life enough to have seen it; felicity had then reached its consummation; the spirit could grasp no more, and the man might end. And what therefore, I ask, must not be in store for the British ratepayer, who in his life has only seen the Duke of Wellington's statue and Coles's truss manufactory? His felicity must surely be yet to come. Somewhere, beyond the grave,' . . . . and for a good twenty minutes my simple friend went on with stuff like this, which I will not weary you with any more of.

I, Sir, as a true Prussian, have a passion for what is *wissenschaftlich* (I do not say 'scientific,' because then you English will think I mean I have an interest in the sea-bear, or in the blue lights and smells of a chemical lecture). I am, I say, *wissenschaftlich;* I love to proceed with the stringency of a philosopher, and Mr. Matthew Arnold with his shillyshallying spoils the ideas I confide to him. Therefore I write to you myself, to tell you (since I like your nation for the sake of the great men it has formerly produced, and of its brave-hearted, industrious people) where the pinch of the matter for you really lies.

It lies here—there is in you '*kein Ernst, der ins Ganze geht.*' You peck at the mere outside of problems; you have not got your mind at work upon them; you fancy they will solve themselves without mind, if only you keep making bottles, and letting every one do what is right in his own eyes, and congratulating yourselves at the top of your voices on your own success. 'Individualism and industrialism will in time replace Coles by a worthier edifice,' says one of your prophets. Not without an '*Ernst der ins Ganze geht,*' I answer. Not without 'Geist' and faith in 'Geist;' and this is just what your individualism and industrialism has not got. 'A self-administering community is surely an ideal.'—That depends entirely on what the self-administering community is like. If it has 'Geist,' and faith in 'Geist,' yes; if it has not, no. Then another of your prophets asks: 'Why should "Geist" care about democracy? Democracy is government by the masses, by the light of their own vulgar tastes.'—Your democracy perhaps, but this is just what makes your weakness; you have no *demos*, no people, but 'masses with vulgar tastes.' The top part of them are in training to be Philistines like your middle-class; the lower part is a rabble. Your democracy has not yet reached even the idea of country; the friends of your northern workmen tell us they read American newspapers, and care more for America than for England. No wonder; they have never been quickened by an '*Ernst der ins Ganze geht*,' the only baptism that makes masses into a people; they have never been in contact with 'Geist,' only with clap-trap. To abate feudalism by providing that in one insignificant case out of one million land shall not follow the feudal law of descent; to abolish English church-rates because the English Dissenters are strong, and to spare the Irish Church Establishment because the Irish Catholics are weak;[1] to give a man leave to marry his

[1] No doubt this remark of Arminius had some share in producing that great measure which has since abolished the Irish Church by the power of the English Dissenters' enmity to Church establishments.—ED.

deceased wife's sister; to give a man who lives in a particular kind of house a vote for members of Parliament—that is the pabulum by which the leaders of your people seek to develop 'Geist' in it, and to awaken an '*Ernst der ins Ganze geht.*' If this is not spiritual enough, as a final resource there is rioting in the parks, and a despotism of your penny newspapers tempered by the tears of your executive, to hasten the growth of English democracy in dignity and intelligence.

The French are not solid enough for my taste; but, *Gott in Himmel!* that people has had a fire baptism, and the democracy which is born of a fire baptism like theirs, 'Geist' cannot help caring about. They were unripe for the task they in '89 set themselves to do; and yet, by the strength of 'Geist' and their faith in 'Geist,' this 'mere viper brood of canting egotists' did so much that they left their trace in half the beneficial reforms through Europe; and if you ask how, at Naples, a convent became a school, or in Ticino an intolerable oligarchy ceased to govern, or in Prussia Stein was able to carry his land-reforms, you get one answer: *the French!* Till modern society is finally formed, French democracy will still be a power in Europe, and it will manage to have effective leaders at the Tuileries, and not only in Cayenne. It will live, though the classes above it may rot; because it has faith in 'Geist,' and does not think that people can do without 'Geist' by dint of holding monster meetings, and having their *Star*[1] and *Telegraph* every morning, and paying no church-rates, and marrying their deceased wife's sister.

We Prussians, Sir, have, as a people, no great love for the French, because we were blown into the air by the explosion of their 'Geist' some sixty years ago, and much quarrelling and ill-blood followed. But we saw then what a power the 'Geist' in their democracy gave them; and we set to work to make ourselves strong, not by a sort of wild fire-baptism of the mass, but in our steady German way, by culture, by *forming* our faculties of all kinds, by every man doing the very best he could with himself, by trusting, with an '*Ernst der ins Ganze geht*,' to mind and not to clap-trap. Your 'earnest Liberal' in England thinks culture all moonshine; he is for the spiritual development of your democracy by rioting in the parks, abolishing church-rates, and marrying a deceased wife's sister; and for leaving your narrow and vulgar middle-class (of which I saw an incomparable specimen in a Reigate train when I was over in England) just as it is. On the other hand, Mr. Matthew

[1] The *Star*, like Arminius himself, has passed from amongst us; but may we not say that its work was done when it had once laid the bases of that admirable and fruitful alliance between Mialism and Millism, which the course of our politics is now every day consolidating?—Ed.

Arnold writes me word that a club has just been formed among you to do honour to the memory of that great man, Richard Cobden; that this club has taken for its motto, 'Peace, Retrenchment, and Reform;' and that these words, by a special command from Mr. Cobden's ghost, are to bear the following interpretation:—'Peace to our nonsense, retrenchment of our profligate expenditure of clap-trap, and reform of ourselves.' Whether this is true, or merely a stroke of my poor friend's so-called playfulness (Heaven save the mark!), I do not feel quite sure; I hope for your sakes it is true, as this is the very thing you want, and nothing else can save you from certain decline.

Do not be astonished at the aristocratic prefix to my name; I come of a family which has for three generations rubbed shoulders with philosophy.

Your humble servant,

VON THUNDER-TEN-TRONCKH.

To

The EDITOR *of the* PALL MALL GAZETTE.

LETTER III.

I expostulate with Arminius on his Revolutionary Sentiments.

SIR,— *Grub Street, August* 6, 1866.

I THOUGHT it was very odd I got no answer from Arminius von Thunder-ten-Tronckh (he was christened Hermann, but I call him Arminius, because it is more in the grand style), when I so particularly begged him to write soon, and save what rags he could of his tissue of nonsense about 'Geist,' after my countrymen had riddled it, as I knew they were sure to do. I suppose he had taken service, like the rest of the German Liberals, under Bismarck, and was too busy pillaging the poor Frankfort people to think of intellectual matters; but I now see he has been writing direct to you, and wants to leave me out in the cold altogether. I do not in the least care for his coarse Prussian sneers, but I must say it is rather good that he should not be above sponging on me week after week in Grub Street, swilling beer (none of your Bavarian wash, but sound English Bass) at my expense, filling my garret (for I don't smoke myself) with the smell of his execrable tobacco, getting the daily benefit of my *Star* and *Telegraph* (I take the *Star* for wisdom and charity, and the *Telegraph* for taste and style), and keeping me up yawning till two o'clock every morning to listen to his rubbishy transcendentalism, and yet be too fine a gentleman to make me the depositary of his ideas for transmission to the English public. But Arminius has the ridiculous pride of his grandfather, who, though the family estate had all gone to the dogs, and he was ruined and turned priest, chose to set his stiff German face against Candide's marriage with his sister. He got shipped off to the Jesuits at Rome, as every one knows; but what is not so well known is,[1] that when the French Revolution came, this precious priest, like Talleyrand, married, and my Arminius is his grandson. Arminius came over here to make acquaintance with Mr. Lowe, who he has found out is in some odd way descended from the philosopher Pangloss,[2] a great friend of the Von Thunder-ten-Tronckh

[1] It was necessarily unknown to Voltaire, who wrote the history of the Von T. family.—Ed.

[2] It is my firm belief that this relationship, which had become a fixed idea with Arminius, never really existed. The optimism of Mr. Lowe's estimate of the British middle class and its House of Commons, in his celebrated speech on Reform, had, in my opinion, struck Arminius's fancy, and made him imagine a kinship in the flesh where there was in truth only a kinship in the spirit. —Ed.

family; but ever since the sack of their château by the Bulgarians, the Von Thunder-ten-Tronckhs have not had a sixpence in the world except what they could get by their 'Geist,' and what Arminius gets by his is such beggar's allowance that he is hardly presentable; well enough for Grub Street, but, as I told him, not at all the sort of company Mr. Lowe keeps.

I don't think Arminius has gained much by being his own expounder, for more vague declamatory trash than his letter I never read. The truth is, he cannot rise to an Englishman's conception of liberty, and understand how liberty, like virtue, is its own reward. 'We go for self-government,' I am always saying to him. 'All right,' he says, 'if it is government by your better self.' 'Fiddlesticks about our better self!' answer I. 'Who is to be the judge? No, the self every man chooses.' 'And what is the self the mass of mankind will choose,' cries he, 'when they are not told there is a better and a worse self, and shown what the better is like?' 'They will choose the worst, very likely,' say I, 'but that is just liberty.' 'And what is to bring good out of such liberty as that?' he asks. 'The glorious and sanative qualities of our matchless Constitution,' I reply; and that is always a stopper for him.

But what I grieve most to observe in Arminius's letter,

and what will lead to my breaking with him in the long run, in spite of my love for intellect, is the bad revolutionary leaven which I see works stronger and stronger in him, and which he no doubt got from the worthless French company his grandfather kept.[1] I noticed an instance of it while he was over here, and I have had another instance, besides his letter to you, since he went away. The instance while he was over here was this. I had taken him down to Wimbledon to see the shooting; and there, walking up and down before the grand tent, was Lord Elcho. Everybody knows Lord Elcho's appearance, and how admirably he looks the part of our governing classes; to my mind, indeed, the mere cock of his lordship's hat is one of the finest and most aristocratic things we have. So of course I pointed Lord Elcho out to Arminius. Arminius eyed him with a jacobinical sort of a smile, and then: 'Cedar of Lebanon which God has not yet broken!' sneered he. I was pleased at Arminius knowing his St. Augustine, for the Prussians are in general thought to be much tainted with irreligion; but I felt at the time, and I feel still, that this was not by any means the proper way of speaking of a dashing nobleman like Lord Elcho.

[1] This partially explains, no doubt, though it cannot altogether excuse, the weak indulgence always cropping out in Arminius for France and its immoral people.—ED.

The other instance is worse still. Besides writing Arminius long letters, I keep him regularly supplied with the *Star*, sending him my own copy after I have read it through twice. I particularly begged him to study the number for last Wednesday week, in which there was the most beautiful account of 'An Aristocratic Reformer.' The other papers had not got it. It related how the Honourable Charles Clifford, a gentleman of strikingly handsome appearance, addressed the crowd in Hyde Park from the footboard of a Hansom. He told them he cared nothing for the Walpoles or Pakingtons, who were for putting down the voice of the people, for, said he, he was higher in social position than they. He was the son of a peer, his son-in-law was a peer, and all his family belonged to the aristocratic classes. This announcement was received with enthusiastic applause by the street-Hampdens present. 'May I ask you, right honourable sir,' cried one of them, 'why, as you are such a big man, you do not open the Park gates to us poor people?' Mr. C. said he wished he had the keys of the Park in his pocket. But he delivered himself of the great principle that it is the duty of the aristocratic classes to protect and promote the interests of the working men, and then he drove off in his Hansom amidst redoubled applause.

Now nothing, Sir, gives me such pride and pleasure as

traits of this kind, which show that we have, as Lord Macaulay finely says, the most popular aristocracy and the most aristocratic people in the world. I thought it would do Arminius good to study the incident, and I wrote him word to that effect. Would you believe it, Sir? Mr. 'Geist' cannot condescend to write me a letter, but he sends me back my *Star* with a vile sketch, or rather caricature, of this touching incident; and opposite Mr. C.'s gentlemanly figure he has written 'Esel,' and opposite the crowd 'Lumpenpack,' which a friend who knows German better than I do tells me are words of disrespect, and even contempt. This is a spirit which I hate and abhor, and I tell Arminius plainly through your columns (since he chooses to adopt this way of corresponding) that unless he can break himself of it all is ended between him and me, and when next he comes to England he will find the garret-door in Grub Street bolted against him.

Your obedient servant,

MATTHEW ARNOLD.

To

The EDITOR *of the* PALL MALL GAZETTE.

LETTER IV.

Arminius assails the British Press for its Free and Independent Comments on Foreign Politics.

SIR,— *Berlin, August* 11, 1866.

FOR Heaven's sake try and prevail upon your countrymen, who are so very anxious for peace for themselves, not to go on biting first the French Emperor's tail and then ours, merely for the fun of the thing apparently, and to have the pleasure of at least seeing a fight between other people, if they cannot have one of their own. You know that Michelet, the French historian, all through his history, familiarly talks of your people as *ce dogue ;* 'upon this *ce dogue mordit* such a one ;' 'upon that *ce dogue déchira* such another.' According to him, you must always be *mordre*-ing or *déchirer*-ing some one, at home or abroad, such is your instinct of savageness ; and you have,—undoubtedly you have,—a strong share of pugnacity. When I was over in England the other day, my poor friend Mr. Matthew Arnold insisted, with his usual blind adoration of everything English, on taking me down to admire one of your great public schools ; precious institutions, where, as I tell him, for 250*l.* sterling a year your boys learn gentlemanly deportment and cricket. Well, down we went, and in the playing-fields (which with you are the school) : 'I declare,' says Mr. Matthew Arnold, 'if there isn't the son of that man you quarrelled with in the Reigate train ! And there, close by him, is a son of one of our greatest families, a Plantagenet ! It is only in England, Arminius, that this beautiful salutary intermixture of classes takes place. Look at the bottle-merchant's son and the Plantagenet being brought up side by side ; none of your absurd separations and seventy-two quarterings here. Very likely young Bottles will end by being a lord himself.' I was going to point out to Mr. Matthew Arnold that what a middle class wants is ideas, and ideas an aristocracy has nothing to do with ; so that that vulgar dog, Bottles the father, in sending his son to learn only cricket and a gentlemanly deportment, like the aristocracy, had done quite the wrong thing with him. But just at this moment our attention was attracted by what was passing between the boys themselves. First, a boy goes up to Bottles, and says : 'Bottles, Plantagenet says he could lick you with one hand ; you are as big as he is,—you wouldn't take a licking from him, would you?' 'No !' answered poor Bottles, rather hesitatingly. Upon this another boy rushes to Plantagenet. 'Plantagenet,' cries he, 'that brute Bottles says he wouldn't take a licking from you.' 'Does he, the beast!' thunders Plantagenet, and, flying at Bottles, hits him full on the nose; and as Bottles's blood streamed out, and I turned away in disgust, I heard the exulting cries of your young 'dogues' making the arrangements for a systematic encounter.

Now really, Sir, since I have been back in Germany your newspapers are perpetually bringing to my mind Michelet's 'dogue' and what I saw in your playing-fields. First you go to the French Emperor, and say: 'Ha, tyrant, we hope humble-pie agrees with you! We hope your tail between your legs is not productive of much inconvenience. Just as the intellectual Emperor was overmatched by an Italian statesman, he now finds himself outdone by a German statesman; a most agreeable thing for an intellectual Emperor—ha! ha! The intellectual Emperor distinctly intimated there must be no disturbing the European equilibrium, else he should interpose. Now the map has been altered enormously to the profit of Prussia, so what is the intellectual Emperor to do? Acknowledge himself outwitted by Count Bismarck, just as he was outwitted by Count Cavour?—ha, ha! Humble-pie! Humble-pie!'— With the greatest alacrity the malcontents in France, the old Constitutional party, take up your parable: 'France is eating humble-pie!' they scream out; 'the tyrant is making

France eat humble pie! France is humiliated! France is suffocating!' France is not difficult to stir up, and the French Emperor has already had to ask for the frontier of 1814. If you go on at this rate I expect he will have to ask for the Mark of Brandenburg next week. Then you will come to Bismarck and say: 'Bismarck, the tyrant is stretching his greedy fist over German soil. Will you let him have it? Think of the prodigious strength you have just shown, of the glory you have just won. Think of French insolence, think of 1813, think of German honour, think of *sauer-kraut*, think of the moral support of England. Not an inch of German soil for the French tyrant!' And so, while you yourselves,—the new man in you, that is,—teach the nations, as Lord Stanley says, how to live, by peacefully developing your bottle-man in the Reigate train, your half-naked starvelings selling matches in St. James's Park, your truss manufactories in Trafalgar Square, and your *Daily Telegraph* saying in spite of all powers human and divine what it likes, you at the same time want to throw a bone to the old 'dogue' in you, in the shape of a very pretty quarrel of your getting up between other people.

Do, Sir, let other people also have a chance of teaching the nations how to live, and emulating your bottle-man and your *Daily Telegraph*. For my part, I have the greatest aversion, and so have all the clearest-headed Germans of my acquaintance, to a quarrel with France. We, as genuine Liberals, know that French democracy is our natural ally. You will observe it is the Constitutionalists in France who are crying out so loudly for more territory to make their strength keep pace with ours. And then think of our poor delicate constitutionalism at home, and of the cruelty of leaving it with its work to do in the face of a war with France, and Bismarck made stronger than ever by such a war! I know our German constitutionalism pretty well. It comes up to the throne, 'With fullest heart-devotion we approach Prussia's King, reverently beseeching him to turn away his unconstitutional ministers.' Prussia's gracious King gives a grunt, and administers a sound kick to his petitioner's behind, who then departs, singing in fervent tones: '*Hoch* for King and fatherland!'

No, Sir; peace, the growth of a republican spirit all through Europe, and a mutual support between all those who share this spirit, are what I wish for. The French are vain; they have been spoilt; we have been going very fast; and you and the Orleanists keep telling them they are humiliated if they do not get something. No doubt people have a right to go to war for the balance of power if they believe in it; you have gone to war for it often enough when it suited your turn. So the Emperor of the French, as you will not let him have a chance of being wise and of seeing that here is a new spiritual force he had not reckoned on, which yet he may perfectly make friends of and live happily with, thinks he must do something for the balance of power; must ask for some rectification or other of frontier. I only hope he will ask for something moderate, and that we shall be moderate when he asks for it. Pray, Sir, pray do not you play the 'dogue' and make moderation harder both for the Emperor and for us.

I assure you a war with France would be a curse to us which even the blessing of your moral support would hardly compensate. And supposing (for certainly you do hate the French pretty strongly) in a year or two you determined to give us your active support,[1] and to send, with infinite crying out, an expedition of fifteen thousand men to the coast of Gothland or some such place, I am afraid,

[1] This is puerile. War between France and Prussia has since happened. We have not been able to give our undivided moral support to either combatant; of our active support, therefore, there could be no question. But it may be fearlessly asserted, that the well-balanced alternations of our moral support, the wise and steady advice given by our newspapers, and, in fact, our attitude generally in regard to this war, have raised Great Britain to a height even more conspicuous than she has ever yet occupied, in the esteem and admiration of foreign countries.—ED.

Sir, with the vast armaments and rapid operations of modern warfare, even this active support of yours would not do us any great good.

Your humble servant,

VON THUNDER-TEN-TRONCKH.

To

The EDITOR *of the* PALL MALL GAZETTE.

P.S.—By the way, I read poor Mr. Matthew Arnold's letter to you the other day. You see just what he is; the discursiveness, the incapacity for arguing, the artlessness, the not very delicate allusions to my private circumstances and his own. It is impossible to enter into any serious discussion with him. But on one point of fact I will set him right. I saw Mr. Lowe and found him very affable; even more like his ancestor Pangloss than I should have thought possible. 'The best of all possible worlds' was always on his lips; 'a system of such tried and tested efficiency;' 'what can we want more?' 'the grumbler fails to suggest even one grievance.' I told him of that bottle barbarian in the Reigate train, and he said that on men of this kind rested 'the mighty fabric of English prosperity.' I could not help saying that in my opinion no country could long stand being ruled by the spirit (or rather matter) of men like that; that a discontent with the present state of things was growing up, and that to-morrow even, or next day, we might see a change. Upon this, Mr. Lowe threw himself into a theatrical attitude, and with the most enthusiastic vehemence exclaimed :—

> To-morrow?
> Oh, spare it, spare it!
> It ought not so to die.[1]

In a man like poor Mr. Matthew Arnold, this infatuation about everything English is conceivable enough, but in a man of Mr. Lowe's parts I own I cannot quite make it out, notwithstanding his descent from Pangloss.

Von T.

[1] As the sentiments here attributed to Mr. Lowe, together with this very remarkable and splendid passage of poetry with which he concludes, are all taken from Mr. Lowe's printed speeches, and may have been read by Arminius in the *Times*, I still retain my doubts whether his interview with Mr. Lowe had ever any existence except in his own fertile imagination.—Ed.

LETTER V.

I communicate a Valuable Exposition, by Arminius, of the System of Tenant-right in Prussia.

SIR,— *Grub Street, November* 8, 1866.

MY love for intellect has made me seek a reconciliation with Arminius, in spite of all I had to complain of in him, and any one who had looked in here to-night might have seen him puffing away at his pipe, and laying down the law just in his old style. He was so immensely tickled at the *Daily Telegraph* calling his poor friend,—artless and obscure garretteer that he knows him to be,—'a high priest of the kid-glove persuasion,'[1] that he has been in a good humour ever since, and to-night he has been giving me some information which I do think, notwithstanding the horrid *animus* he betrays in delivering it, is highly curious and interesting, and therefore I hasten to communicate it to you.

[1] Besides all I had to endure from Arminius himself, our leading newspapers persisted in holding me answerable for every paradox uttered by him.—ED.

It is about the Prussian land reforms, and this is how I got it out of him. 'You made me look rather a fool, Arminius,' I began, 'by what you primed me with in Germany last year about Stein settling your land question.' 'I dare say you looked a fool,' says my Prussian boor, 'but what did I tell you?' 'Why,' says I, 'you told me Stein had settled a land question like the Irish land question, and I said so in the *Cornhill Magazine*, and now the matter has come up again by Mr. Bright talking at Dublin of what Stein did, and it turns out he settled nothing like the Irish land question at all, but only a sort of tithe-commutation affair.' 'Who says that?' asked Arminius. 'A very able writer in the *Times*,' I replied.

I don't know that I have ever described Arminius's personal appearance. He has the true square Teutonic head, a blond and disorderly mass of tow-like hair, a podgy and sanguine countenance, shaven cheeks, and a whity-brown moustache. He wears a rough pilot-coat, and generally smokes away with his hands in the pockets of it, and his light blue eyes fixed on his interlocutor's face. When he takes his hands out of his pockets, his pipe out of his mouth, and his eyes off his friend's face, it is a sign that he is deeply moved. He did all this on the present occasion, and passing his short thick fingers two or three times through his blond hair: 'That astonishing paper!' muttered he.

Then he began as solemn as if he was in a pulpit. 'My dear friend,' says he, 'of the British species of the great genus Philistine there are three main varieties. There is the religious Philistine, the well-to-do Philistine, and the rowdy Philistine. The religious Philistine is represented by——' 'Stop, Arminius,' said I, 'you will oblige me by letting religion alone!' 'As you please,' answered he; 'well, then, the rowdy Philistine is represented by the *Daily Telegraph*, and the well-to-do Philistine by the *Times*. The well-to-do Philistine looks to get his own view of the British world,—that it is the best of all possible worlds as it is, because he has prospered in it,—preached back to him *ore rotundo* in the columns of the *Times*. There must be no uncertain sound in his oracle, no faltering, nothing to excite misgivings or doubts; like his own bosom, everything his oracle utters must be positive, pleasant, and comfortable. So of course about the great first article of his creed, the sacro-sanctity of property, there must in the *Times* be no trifling. But what amuses me is that his oracle must not even admit, if these matters come to be talked of, that Stein trifled with it in another country. The ark is so sacred, the example so abominable, and the devotee so sensitive. And therefore Stein's reforms become in the *Times*, for the reassurance of the well-to-do British Philistine, a sort of tithe-commutation affair,—nothing in the world more! nothing in the world more!'

'Don't go on in that absurd way, Arminius,' said I; 'I don't tell you it was a tithe-commutation, but a commutation like the tithe-commutation. It was simply, the *Times* says, the conversion of serf-tenures into produce-rents. I hope that gives you a perfectly clear notion of what the whole thing was, for it doesn't me. But I make out from the *Times* that the *leibeigener*——' 'Rubbish about the *leibeigener*,' cries Arminius, in a rage, 'and all this jargon to keep your stupid mind in a mist; do you want to know what really happened?' 'Yes, I do,' said I, quietly, my love for knowledge making me take no notice of his impertinence. 'Yes, I do, and particularly this: In the first place, was the land, before Stein's reforms, the landlord's or the tenant's?' 'The landlord's,' says Arminius. 'You mean,' said I, 'that the landlord could and did really eject his tenant from it if he chose.' 'Yes, I do,' says Arminius. 'Well, then, what did Stein do?' asked I. 'He did this,' Arminius answered. 'In these estates, where the landlord had his property-right on the one hand, and the tenant his tenant-right on the other, he made a compromise. In the first place he assigned, say, two-fifths of the estate to the landlord in absolute property, without any further claim of tenant-right upon it thenceforth for ever. But the remaining three-fifths he compelled the landlord to sell to the tenant at eighteen years' purchase, so that this part should become the tenant's absolute property thenceforth for ever. You will ask, where could the tenant find money to buy? Stein opened rent-banks in all the provincial chief towns, to lend the tenant the purchase-money required, for which the State thus became his creditor, not the landlord. He had to repay this loan in a certain number of years. To free his land from this State mortgage on it and make it his own clear property, he had every inducement to work hard, and he did work hard; and this was the grand source of the frugality, industry, and thrivingness of the Prussian peasant. It was the grand source, too, of his attachment to the State.' 'It was rotten bad political economy, though,' exclaimed I. 'Now I see what the *Times* meant by saying in its leading article yesterday that Ireland is incomparably better governed than the United States, France, Germany, or Italy, because the excellence of government consists in keeping obstacles out of the way of individual energy, and you throw obstacles in the way of your great proprietors' energy, and we throw none in the way of ours. Talk of a commutation like the tithe-commutation, indeed! Why it was downright spoliation;

it was just what Lord Clanricarde says some people are driving at in Ireland, a system of confiscation.' 'Well,' says Arminius, calmly, 'that is exactly what the Prussian junkers called it. They did not call it commutation, they called it confiscation. They will tell you to this day that Stein confiscated their estates. But you will be shocked to hear that the Prussian Government had, even before Stein's time, this sad habit of playing tricks with political economy. To prevent the absorption of small proprietors by a great landed aristocracy, the Prussian Government made a rule that a *bauer-gut*,—a peasant property,—could not, even if the owner sold it, be bought up by the Lord Clanricarde of the neighbourhood; it must remain a *bauer-gut* still. I believe you in England are for improving small proprietors off the face of the earth, but I assure you in Prussia we are very proud of ours, and think them the strength of the nation. Of late years the Hohenzollerns have taken up with the junkers, but for a long time their policy was to uphold the *bauer* class against the *junker* class; and, if you want to know the secret of the hold which the house of Hohenzollern has upon the heart of the Prussian people, it is not in Frederick the Great's victories that you will find it, it is in this policy of their domestic government.' 'My dear Arminius,' said I, 'you make me perfectly sick. Government here, government there! We English are for self-government. What business has any Mr. Stein to settle that this or that estate is too large for Lord Clanricarde's virtues to expand in? Let each class settle its own affairs, and don't let us have Governments and Hohenzollerns pretending to be more enlightened than other people, and cutting and carving for what they call the general interest, and God knows what nonsense of that kind. If the landed class with us has got the magistracy and settled estates and game laws, has not the middle class got the vestries, and business, and civil and religious liberty? I remember when the late Sir George Cornewall Lewis wanted to get some statistics about the religious denominations, your friend Bottles, who is now a millionaire and a Churchman, was then a Particular Baptist. "No," says Bottles, "here I put down my foot. No Government on earth shall ask me whether I am a Particular Baptist or a Muggletonian." And Bottles beat the Government, because of the thorough understanding the upper and middle classes in this country have with one another that each is to go its own way, and Government is not to be thrusting its nose into the concerns of either. There is a cordial alliance between them on this basis.' 'Yes, yes, I know,' Arminius sneeringly answered; 'Herod and Pontius Pilate have shaken hands.'

'But I will show you, Arminius,' I pursued, 'on plain grounds of political economy——' 'Not to-night,' interrupted Arminius, yawning; 'I am going home to bed.' And off he went, descending the garret stairs three at a time, and leaving me to burn the midnight-oil in order to send you, Sir, what is really, I flatter myself, an interesting, and I may even say a valuable, communication.

Your humble servant,

MATTHEW ARNOLD.

To

The EDITOR *of the* PALL MALL GAZETTE.

LETTER VI.

I become intrusted with the Views of Arminius on Compulsory Education.

SIR,— *Grub Street, April 20, 1867.*

IT is a long while since you have heard anything of Arminius and me, though I do hope you have sometimes given a thought to us both. The truth is we have been in the country. You may imagine how horribly disagreeable Arminius made himself during the famous snow in London at the beginning of this year. About the state of the streets he was bad enough, but about the poor frozen-out working men who went singing without let or hindrance before our houses, he quite made my blood creep. 'The dirge of a society *qui s'en va*,' he used to call their pathetic songs. It is true I had always an answer for him—'Thank God, we are not Hausmannised yet!' and if that was not enough, and he wanted the philosophy of the thing, why I turned to a sort of constitutional commonplace book, or true Englishman's *vade mecum*, which I have been these many years forming for my own use by potting extracts from the *Times* and which I hope one day to give to the world, and I read him this golden aphorism: 'Administrative, military, and clerical tyranny are unknown in this country, because the educated class discharges all the corresponding functions through committees of its own body.' 'Well, then,' Arminius would answer, 'show me your administrative committee for ridding us of these cursed frozen-out impostors.' 'My dear Arminius,' was my quiet reply, 'voluntary organisations are not to be dealt with in this peremptory manner. The administrative committee you ask for will develop itself in good time; its future members are probably now at nurse. In England we like our improvements to *grow*, not to be manufactured.'

However the mental strain, day after day, of this line of high constitutional argument was so wearing, that I gladly acceded to a proposal made by Arminius in one of his fits of grumbling to go with him for a little while into the country. So into the country we went, and there, under his able guidance, I have been assiduously pursuing the study of German philosophy. As a rule, I attend to nothing else just now; but when we were taking one of our walks abroad the other morning, an incident happened which led us to discuss the subject of compulsory education, and, as this subject is beginning to awaken deep interest in the public mind, I think you may be glad to have an account of the incident, and of the valuable remarks on compulsory education which were drawn from Arminius by it.

We were going out the other morning on one of our walks, as I said, when we saw a crowd before the inn of the country town where we have been staying. It was the magistrates' day for sitting, and I was glad of an opportunity to show off our local self-government to a bureaucracy-ridden Prussian like Arminius. So I stopped in the crowd, and there we saw an old fellow in a smock-frock, with a white head, a low forehead, a red nose, and a foxy expression of countenance, being taken along to the justice-room. Seeing among the bystanders a contributor to the *Daily Telegraph*,[1] whom I formerly knew well enough,—for he had the drawing-room floor underneath me in Grub Street, but the magnificent circulation of that journal has long since carried him, like the course of empire, westward,—I asked him if he could tell me what the prisoner was charged with. I found it was a hardened old poacher, called Diggs,—Zephaniah Diggs,—and that he was had up for snaring a hare,—probably his ten-

[1] Do you recognise yourself, Leo? Is it presumptuous in me, upon giving this volume to the world, to bid you too, my friend, say with the poet: *Non omnis moriar?*—ED.

thousandth. The worst of the story, to my mind, was that the old rogue had a heap of young children by a second wife whom he had married late in life, and that not one of these children would he send to school, but persisted in letting them all run wild, and grow up in utter barbarism.

I hastened to tell Arminius that it was a poaching case; and I added that it was not always, perhaps, in poaching cases that our local self-government appeared to the best advantage. 'In the present case, however, there is,' said I, 'no danger; for a representative of the *Daily Telegraph* is down here, to be on the look-out for justices' justice, and to prevent oppression.' Immediately afterwards I was sorry I had said this, for there are unfortunately several things which operate on Arminius like scarlet on a bull, making him vicious the moment he comes across them; and the *Daily Telegraph* is one of these things. He declares it foments our worst faults; and he is fond of applying to it Dryden's dictum on Elkanah Settle, that its style is boisterous and its prose incorrigibly lewd. Though I do certainly think its prose a little full-bodied, yet I cannot bear to hear Arminius apply such a term to it as 'incorrigibly lewd;' and I always remonstrate with him. 'No, Arminius,' I always say, 'I hope not *incorrigibly*; I should be sorry to think that of a publication which is forming the imagination and taste of millions of Englishmen.' 'Pleasant news,' was Arminius's answer, the last time I urged this to him, 'pleasant news ; the next batch of you, then, will be even more charming than the present!'

I trouble you with all this, Sir, to account for the acerbity of tone in some of Arminius's subsequent conversation; an acerbity he too often manifests, and which tends, as I tell him, to detract from the influence which his talents and acquirements would otherwise give him. On the present occasion he took no direct notice of my mention of the *Daily Telegraph*, but seemed quite taken up with scrutinising old Diggs. 'Such a peasant as that wretched old creature,' he said at last, 'is peculiar, my dear friend, to your country. Only look at that countenance! Centuries of feudalism have effaced in it every gleam of humane life.' . . . 'Centuries of fiddlesticks!' interrupted I (for I assure you, Sir, I can stand up to Arminius well enough on a proper occasion). 'My dear Arminius, how can you allow yourself to talk such rubbish? Gleam of humane life, indeed! do but look at the twinkle in the old rogue's eye. He has plenty of life and wits about him, has old Diggs, I can assure you; you just try and come round him about a pot of beer!' 'The mere cunning of an animal!' retorted Arminius. 'For my part,' pursued I, 'it is his children I think most about; I am told not one of them has ever seen the inside of a school. Do you know, Arminius, I begin to think, and many people in this country begin to think, that the time has almost come for taking a leaf out of your Prussian book, and applying, in the education of children of this class, what the great Kant calls the categorical imperative. The gap between them and our educated and intelligent classes is really too frightful.' 'Your educated and intelligent classes!' sneered Arminius, in his very most offensive manner; 'where are they? I should like to see them.'

I was not going to stand and hear our aristocracy and middle-class set down in this way; so, treating Arminius's ebullition of spite as beneath my notice, I pushed my way through the crowd to the inn-door. I asked the policeman there what magistrates were on the bench to day. 'Viscount Lumpington,' says the man, 'Reverend Esau Hittall, and Bottles Esquire.' 'Good heavens!' I exclaimed, turning round to Arminius, who had followed me, and forgetting, in my excitement, my just cause of offence with him,—'Good heavens, Arminius, if Bottles hasn't got himself made a county magistrate! *Sic itur ad astra.*' 'Yes,' says Arminius, with a smile, 'one of your educated and intelligent classes, I suppose. And I dare say the other two are to match. Your magistrates are a sort of judges, I know; just the people who are drawn from the educated and intelligent classes. Now, what's sauce for the goose is sauce for the gander; if you put a pressure on one class to make it train itself properly, you must put a pressure on others to the same end. That is what we do in Prussia, if you are going to take a leaf out of our book. I want to hear what steps you take to put this pressure on people above old Diggs there, and then I will talk to you about putting it on old Diggs. Take his judges who are going to try him to-day; how about them? What training have you made them give themselves, and what are their qualifications?'

I luckily happen to know Lord Lumpington and Hittall pretty well, having been at college with them in former days, when I little thought the Philistines would have brought my grey hairs to a garret in Grub Street; and I have made the acquaintance of Mr. Bottles since, and know all about him. So I was able to satisfy Arminius's curiosity, and I had great pleasure in making him remark, as I did so, the rich diversity of our English life, the healthy natural play of our free institutions, and the happy blending of classes and characters which this promotes. 'The three magistrates in that inn,' said I, 'are not three Government functionaries all cut out of one block; they embody our whole national life;—the land, religion, commerce, are all represented by them. Lord Lumpington is a peer of old family and great estate; Esau Hittall is a clergyman; Mr.

Bottles is one of our self-made middle-class men. Their politics are not all of one colour, and that colour the Government's. Lumpington is a Constitutional Whig; Hittall is a benighted old Tory. As for Mr. Bottles, he is a Radical of the purest water; quite one of the Manchester school. He was one of the earliest free-traders; he has always gone as straight as an arrow about Reform; he is an ardent voluntary in every possible line, opposed the Ten Hours' Bill, was one of the leaders of the Dissenting opposition out of Parliament which smashed up the education clauses of Sir James Graham's Factory Act; and he paid the whole expenses of a most important church-rate contest out of his own pocket. And, finally, he looks forward to marrying his deceased wife's sister. Table, as my friend Mr. Grant Duff says, the whole Liberal creed, and in not a single point of it will you find Bottles tripping!'

'That is all very well as to their politics,' said Arminius, 'but I want to hear about their education and intelligence.' 'There, too, I can satisfy you,' I answered. 'Lumpington was at Eton. Hittall was on the foundation at Charterhouse, placed there by his uncle, a distinguished prelate, who was one of the trustees. You know we English have no notion of your bureaucratic tyranny of treating the appointments to these great foundations as public patronage, and vesting them in a responsible minister; we vest them in independent magnates, who relieve the State of all work and responsibility, and never take a shilling of salary for their trouble. Hittall was the last of six nephews nominated to the Charterhouse by his uncle, this good prelate, who had thoroughly learnt the divine lesson that charity begins at home.' 'But I want to know what his nephew learnt,' interrupted Arminius, 'and what Lord Lumpington learnt at Eton.' 'They followed,' said I, 'the grand, old, fortifying, classical curriculum.' 'Did they know anything when they left?' asked Arminius. 'I have seen some longs and shorts of Hittall's,' said I, 'about the Calydonian Boar, which were not bad. But you surely don't need me to tell you, Arminius, that it is rather in training and bracing the mind for future acquisition,—a course of mental gymnastics we call it,—than in teaching any set thing, that the classical curriculum is so valuable.' 'Were the minds of Lord Lumpington and Mr. Hittall much braced by their mental gymnastics?' inquired Arminius. 'Well,' I answered, 'during their three years at Oxford they were so much occupied with Bullingdon and hunting that there was no great opportunity to judge. But for my part I have always thought that their both getting their degree at last with flying colours, after three weeks of a famous coach for fast men, four nights without going to bed, and an incredible consumption of wet towels, strong cigars, and brandy-and-water, was one of the most astonishing feats of mental gymnastics I ever heard of.'

'That will do for the land and the Church,' said Arminius. 'And now let us hear about commerce.' 'You mean how was Bottles educated?' answered I. 'Here we get into another line altogether, but a very good line in its way, too. Mr. Bottles was brought up at the Lycurgus House Academy, Peckham. You are not to suppose from the name of Lycurgus that any Latin and Greek was taught in the establishment; the name only indicates the moral discipline, and the strenuous earnest character, imparted there. As to the instruction, the thoughtful educator who was principal of the Lycurgus House Academy,—Archimedes Silverpump, Ph.D., you must have heard of him in Germany?—had modern views. "We must be men of our age," he used to say. "Useful knowledge, living languages, and the forming of the mind through observation and experiment, these are the fundamental articles of my educational creed." Or, as I have heard his pupil Bottles put it in his expansive moments after dinner (Bottles used to ask me to dinner till that affair of yours with him in the Reigate train): "Original man, Silverpump! fine mind! fine system! None of your antiquated rubbish—all practical work—latest discoveries in science—mind constantly kept excited—lots of interesting experiments—lights of all colours—fizz! fizz! bang! bang! That's what I call forming a man."'

'And pray,' cried Arminius, impatiently, 'what sort of man do you suppose this infernal quack really formed in your precious friend Mr. Bottles?' 'Well,' I replied, 'I hardly know how to answer that question. Bottles has certainly made an immense fortune; but as to Silverpump's effect on his mind, whether it was from any fault in the Lycurgus House system, whether it was that with a sturdy self-reliance thoroughly English, Bottles, ever since he quitted Silverpump, left his mind wholly to itself, his daily newspaper, and the Particular Baptist minister under whom he sate, or from whatever cause it was, certainly his mind, *quâ* mind —' 'You need not go on,' interrupted Arminius, with a magnificent wave of his hand, 'I know what that man's mind, *quâ* mind, is, well enough.'

But, Sir, the midnight oil is beginning to run very low; I hope, therefore, you will permit me to postpone the rest of Arminius's discourse till to-morrow. And meanwhile, Sir, I am, with all respect,

Your humble servant,

MATTHEW ARNOLD.

To

The EDITOR *of the* PALL MALL GAZETTE.

LETTER VII.

More about Compulsory Education.

SIR,— *Grub Street, April* 21, 1867.

I TAKE up the thread of the interesting and important discussion on compulsory education between Arminius and me where I left it last night.

'But,' continued Arminius, 'you were talking of compulsory education, and your common people's want of it. Now, my dear friend, I want you to understand what this principle of compulsory education really means. It means that to ensure, as far as you can, every man's being fit for his business in life, you put education as a bar, or condition, between him and what he aims at. The principle is just as good for one class as another, and it is only by applying it impartially that you save its application from being insolent and invidious. Our Prussian peasant stands our compelling him to instruct himself before he may go about his calling, because he sees we believe in instruction, and compel our own class, too, in a way to make it really feel the pressure, to instruct itself before it may go about its calling. Now, you propose to make old Diggs's boys instruct themselves before they may go bird-scaring or sheep-tending. I want to know what you do to make those three worthies in that justice-room instruct themselves before they may go acting as magistrates and judges.' 'Do?' said I; 'why, just look what they have done all of themselves. Lumpington and Hittall have had a public-school and university education; Bottles has had Dr. Silverpump's, and the practical training of business. What on earth would you have us make them do more?' 'Qualify themselves for administrative or judicial functions, if they exercise them,' said Arminius. 'That is what really answers, in their case, to the compulsion you propose to apply to Diggs's boys. Sending Lord Lumpington and Mr. Hittall to school is nothing; the natural course of things takes them there. Don't suppose that, by doing this, you are applying the principle of compulsory education fairly, and as you apply it to Diggs's boys. You are not interposing, for the rich, education as a bar or condition between them and that which they aim at. But interpose it, as we do, between the rich and things they aim at, and I will say something to you. I should like to know what has made Lord Lumpington a magistrate?' 'Made Lord Lumpington a magistrate?' said I; 'why, the Lumpington estate, to be sure.' 'And the Reverend

Esau Hittall?' continued Arminius. 'Why, the Lumpington living, of course,' said I. 'And that man Bottles?' he went on. 'His English energy and self-reliance,' I answered very stiffly, for Arminius's incessant carping began to put me in a huff; 'those same incomparable and truly British qualities which have just triumphed over every obstacle and given us the Atlantic telegraph!—and let me tell you, Von T., in my opinion it will be a long time before the "Geist" of any pedant of a Prussian professor gives us anything half so valuable as that.' 'Pshaw!' replied Arminius, contemptuously; 'that great rope, with a Philistine at each end of it talking inutilities!

'But in my country,' he went on, 'we should have begun to put a pressure on these future magistrates at school. Before we allowed Lord Lumpington and Mr. Hittall to go to the university at all, we should have examined them, and we should not have trusted the keepers of that absurd cockpit you took me down to see, to examine them as they chose, and send them jogging comfortably off to the university on their lame longs and shorts. No; there would have been some Mr. Grote as School Board Commissary, pitching into them questions about history, and some Mr. Lowe, as Crown Patronage Commissary, pitching into them questions about English literature; and these young men would have been kept from the university, as Diggs's boys are kept from their bird-scaring, till they had instructed themselves. Then, if, after three years of their university, they wanted to be magistrates, another pressure!—a great Civil Service examination before a board of experts, an examination in English law, Roman law, English history, history of jurisprudence——' 'A most abominable liberty to take with Lumpington and Hittall!' exclaimed I. 'Then your compulsory education is a most abominable liberty to take with Diggs's boys,' retorted Arminius. 'But, good gracious! my dear Arminius,' expostulated I, 'do you really mean to maintain that a man can't put old Diggs in quod for snaring a hare without all this elaborate apparatus of Roman law and history of jurisprudence?' 'And do you really mean to maintain,' returned Arminius, 'that a man can't go bird-scaring or sheep-tending without all this elaborate apparatus of a compulsory school?' 'Oh, but,' I answered, 'to live at all, even at the lowest stage of human life, a man needs instruction.' 'Well,' returned Arminius, 'and to administer at all, even at the lowest stage of public administration, a man needs instruction.' 'We have never found it so,' said I.

Arminius shrugged his shoulders and was silent. By this time the proceedings in the justice-room were drawn to an end, the majesty of the law had been vindicated against old Diggs, and the magistrates were coming out. I never saw a finer spectacle than my friend Arminius presented, as he stood by to gaze on the august trio as they passed. His pilot-coat was tightly buttoned round his stout form, his light blue eye shone, his sanguine cheeks were ruddier than ever with the cold morning and the excitement of discourse, his fell of tow was blown about by the March wind, and volumes of tobacco-smoke issued from his lips. So in old days stood, I imagine, his great namesake by the banks of the Lippe, glaring on the Roman legions before their destruction.

Lord Lumpington was the first who came out. His lordship good-naturedly recognised me with a nod, and then eyeing Arminius with surprise and curiosity: 'Whom on earth have you got there?' he whispered. 'A very distinguished young Prussian *savant*,' replied I; and then dropping my voice, in my most impressive undertones I added: 'And a young man of very good family, besides, my lord.' Lord Lumpington looked at Arminius again; smiled, shook his head, and then, turning away, and half aloud: 'Can't compliment you on your friend,' says he.

As for that centaur Hittall, who thinks of nothing on earth but field-sports, and in the performance of his sacred duties never warms up except when he lights on some passage about hunting or fowling, he always, whenever he meets me, remembers that in my unregenerate days, before Arminius inoculated me with a passion for intellect, I was rather fond of shooting, and not quite such a successful shot as Hittall himself. So, the moment he catches sight of me: 'How d'ye do, old fellow?' he blurts out; 'well, been shooting any straighter this year than you used to, eh?'

I turned from him in pity, and then I noticed Arminius, who had unluckily heard Lord Lumpington's unfavourable comment on him, absolutely purple with rage and blowing like a turkeycock. 'Never mind, Arminius,' said I soothingly; 'run after Lumpington, and ask him the square root of thirty-six.' But now it was my turn to be a little annoyed, for at the same instant Mr. Bottles stepped into his brougham, which was waiting for him, and observing Arminius, his old enemy of the Reigate train, he took no notice whatever of me who stood there, with my hat in my hand, practising all the airs and graces I have learnt on the Continent; but, with that want of amenity I so often have to deplore in my countrymen, he pulled up the glass on our side with a grunt and a jerk, and drove off like the wind, leaving Arminius in a very bad temper indeed, and me, I confess, a good deal shocked and mortified.

However, both Arminius and I got over it, and have now returned to London, where I hope we shall before long have another good talk about educational matters. Whatever Arminius may say, I am still for going straight, with all our heart and soul, at compulsory education for the lower orders. Why, good heavens ! Sir, with our present squeezable Ministry, we are evidently drifting fast to household suffrage, pure and simple; and I observe, moreover, a Jacobinical spirit growing up in some quarters which gives me more alarm than even household suffrage. My elevated position in Grub Street, Sir, where I sit commercing with the stars, commands a view of a certain spacious and secluded back yard; and in that back yard, Sir, I tell you confidentially that I saw the other day with my own eyes that powerful young publicist, Mr. Frederic Harrison, in full evening costume, furbishing up a guillotine. These things are very serious ; and I say, if the masses are to have power, let them be instructed, and don't swamp with ignorance and unreason the education and intelligence which now bear rule amongst us. For my part, when I think of Lumpington's estate, family, and connections, when I think of Hittall's shooting, and of the energy and self-reliance of Bottles, and when I see the unexampled pitch of splendour and security to which these have conducted us, I am bent, I own, on trying to make the new elements of our political system worthy of the old; and I say kindly, but firmly, to the compound householder in the French poet's beautiful words,[1] slightly altered: 'Be great, O working class, for the middle and upper class are great!'

I am, Sir,

Your humble servant,

MATTHEW ARNOLD.

To

The EDITOR *of the* PALL MALL GAZETTE.

[1] 'Et tâchez d'être grand, car le peuple grandit.'

(FROM the autumn of this year (1867) dates one of the most painful memories of my life. I have mentioned in the last letter but one how in the spring I was commencing the study of German philosophy with Arminius. In the autumn of that year the celebrated young Comtist, Mr. Frederic Harrison, resenting some supposed irreverence of mine towards his master, permitted himself, in a squib, brilliant indeed, but unjustifiably severe, to make game of my inaptitude for philosophical pursuits. It was on this occasion he launched the damning sentence: 'We seek vainly in Mr. A. a system of philosophy with principles coherent, interdependent, subordinate, and derivative.' The blow came at an unlucky moment for me. I was studying, as I have said, German philosophy with Arminius; we were then engaged on Hegel's 'Phenomenology of *Geist*,' and it was my habit to develop to Arminius, at great length, my views of the meaning of his great but difficult countryman. One morning I had, perhaps, been a little fuller than usual over a very profound chapter. Arminius was suffering from dyspepsia (brought on, as I believe, by incessant smoking); his temper, always irritable, seemed suddenly to burst from all control,—he flung the *Phänomenologie* to the other end of the room, exclaiming: 'That smart young fellow is quite right! it is impossible to make a silk purse out of a sow's ear!' This led to a rupture, in which I think I may fairly say that the chief blame was not on my side. But two invaluable years were thus lost; Arminius abandoned me for Mr. Frederic Harrison, who must certainly have many memoranda of his later conversations, but has never given them, as I always did mine of his earlier ones, to the world. A melancholy occasion brought Arminius and me together again in 1869; the sparkling pen of my friend Leo has luckily preserved the record of what then passed.)—Ed.

LETTER VIII.

Under a Playful Signature, my Friend Leo, of the 'Daily Telegraph,' advocates an important Liberal Measure, and, in so doing, gives News of Arminius.

SIR,— *St. James's Place, June 8, 1869.*

FOR the sake of my health it is my custom at this full-blooded time of the year to submit myself to a lowering course of medical treatment, which causes me for a few days to be voted below par for Fleet Street; so I have bethought myself of utilising my leisure, while universal humanity does not claim me, and while my style is reduced nearer the pitch of the *Pall Mall Gazette*, by writing to you on a subject in which I am strongly interested, and on which your ideas are, I am sorry to see, far from sound. I mean that great subject of which a fragment will be brought under discussion to-night, by the House of Commons going into Committee on Mr. Chambers's admirable bill for enabling a woman to marry her sister's husband.

My ideas on this subject have been stirred into lively activity by a visit I have just been making. I believe my name has been once or twice mentioned in your columns in connection with the Bottles family near Reigate, and with a group of friends gathered round them. Poor Mrs. Bottles, I grieve to say, is not long for this world. She and her family showed an interest in me while I was rising to name and fame, and I trust I have never forgotten it. She sate, as Curran says, by my cradle, and I intend to follow her hearse. Meanwhile, with our Paris correspondent, who happens to be over here for a few days, I have been down to Reigate to inquire after her. The accounts were unhappily as bad as possible; but what I saw awakened a train of ideas and suggestions which I am going to communicate to you.

I found a good many people assembled, of whom several had come on the same errand as I. There was that broken-down acquaintance of my early youth, Mr. Matthew Arnold, who has had many a dinner from Mrs. Bottles (for she was kind to literature even in its humblest manifestations), snivelling and crying in a corner. There was that offensive young Prussian of his, who seems to have dropped him entirely, and to have taken up with a much younger man than my poor old acquaintance, and a much better-dressed man, with whom he is pursuing researches concerning labour and capital, which are hardly, as our Paris correspondent says, palpitating with actuality.

There was a Baptist minister who had been the shepherd of the Bottles family in the old days when they were Dissenters, and who has never quite lost his hold upon Mrs. Bottles. There was her sister Hannah, just about the same age as poor Sarah who married Bottles, and the very image of her. There was Job Bottles, Bottles's brother, who is on the Stock Exchange; a man with black hair at the sides of his head, a bald crown, dark eyes and a fleshy nose, and a camellia in his button-hole. Finally, there was that handsome niece of Mr. and Mrs. Bottles, Mary Jane. *Mary Jane!* I never pronounce the name without emotion; in season and out of season it keeps rising to my lips.[1] But the life we live in Fleet Street is devouring, and I have sacrificed to it all thought of marriage. Our Paris correspondent comforts me by saying that, even with the domestic affections suppressed, existence turns out to be a much more tolerable affair than humdrum people fancy.

Presently the members of the family left the room, and as the Baptist minister took the *Nonconformist* out of his pocket and began to read it, as the Prussian savant was quite absorbed with his new young man, and as Mr.

[1] Leo here alludes, I imagine, to what the world has doubtless noticed,—the frequent introduction of *Mary Jane* into his articles for the *D. T.*—ED.

Matthew Arnold counts for nothing, I was left to the conversation of our Paris correspondent, whom we call Nick because of the diabolical salt which sparkles in his deliverances. 'They say,' I began, 'that if Mr. T. Chambers's excellent bill, which the Liberal party are carrying with such decisive majorities, becomes law, the place of poor Mrs. Bottles will be taken by her sister Hannah, whom you have just seen. Nothing could be more proper; Mrs. Bottles wishes it, Miss Hannah wishes it, this reverend friend of the family, who has himself made a marriage of the same kind, wishes it, everybody wishes it.' 'Everybody but old Bottles himself, I should think,' retorted my friend; 'don't envy him at all!—shouldn't so much mind if it were the younger one, though.'

These light words of my friend, Sir, seemed to touch a spring in me. Instantly I felt myself visited by a shower of ideas, full of import for the Liberal party and for the future, and which impel me to address to you the present letter. 'And why not the younger one, Nick?' said I, gently: 'why not? Either as a successor to Miss Hannah or in lieu of Miss Hannah, why not? Let us apply John Bright's crucial tests. Is she his first cousin? Could there be a more natural companion for Selina and the other Bottles girls? Or,—to take the moral ground so touchingly and irresistibly chosen by our great popular tribune,—if legislation on this subject were impeded by the party of bigotry, if they chose not to wait for it, if they got married without it, and if you were to meet them on the boulevard at Paris during their wedding tour, should you go up to Bottles and say: Mr. Bottles, you are a profligate man?' 'Oh dear, no,' said Nick; 'I should never dream of it.' 'And if you met them a year later on the same spot,' I continued, 'with a Normandy nurse behind them carrying a baby, should you cry out to the poor little thing: Bastard?' 'Nothing of the kind,' he answered.

I noticed that my friend accompanied each of these assurances with a slight rapid droop of one eyelid. 'Let us have no flippancy, Nick,' I said. 'You mean that you hardly feel yourself in a position to take high moral ground of this kind.' 'Well,' said he, 'I suppose that even our great tribune, John Bright himself, does not very often address people as bastards and profligates, whatever he thinks of them. At least, I should imagine the offender must almost be a bishop or some other high-placed Anglican ecclesiastic to provoke him to do so.' 'A fig for your fine distinctions,' cried I. 'Secretly or openly, will any one dare call Bottles, if he contracts a marriage of this kind, a profligate man?'

Poor Mr. Matthew Arnold, upon this, emerged suddenly from his corner, and asked hesitatingly: 'But will any one dare call him a man of delicacy?' The question was so utterly unpractical that I took no notice of it whatever, and should not have mentioned it if it had not led, by its extraordinary effect upon our Paris correspondent, to the introduction and criticism of a literary star of the first magnitude. My friend Nick, who has all the sensitive temperament of genius, seemed inexplicably struck by this word delicacy, which he kept repeating to himself. 'Delicacy,' said he, 'delicacy,—surely I have heard that word before! Yes, in other days,' he went on dreamily, 'in my fresh, enthusiastic youth; before I knew Sala, before I wrote for that infernal paper, before I called Dixon's style lithe and sinewy——'

'Collect yourself, my friend,' said I, laying my hand on his shoulder; 'you are unmanned. But in mentioning Dixon you redouble my strength; for you bring to my mind the great sexual insurrection of the Anglo-Teutonic race, and the master-spirit which guides it. This illustrious man, who has invented a new style——'

'He has, indeed,' says Mr. Arminius, the Prussian, turning towards us for the first time; 'he has, indeed, and its right name is middle-class Macaulayese.'

Now, I detest this German lecturer and his oracles, but as I am, above everything, a man of letters myself,

I never refuse to listen to a remark upon style. 'Explain yourself,' said I; 'why do you call Mr. Hepworth Dixon's style middle-class Macaulayese?' 'I call it Macaulayese,' says the pedant, 'because it has the same internal and external characteristics as Macaulay's style; the external characteristic being a hard metallic movement with nothing of the soft play of life, and the internal characteristic being a perpetual semblance of hitting the right nail on the head without the reality. And I call it middle-class Macaulayese, because it has these faults without the compensation of great studies and of conversance with great affairs, by which Macaulay partly redeemed them.'

I turned away in pity. 'Let us leave the envious,' said I to Nick, 'to break their teeth on this magnificent file, the countlessness of whose editions has something analogous to the world-wide circulation of the *Daily Telegraph.* Let us pursue his fine regenerating idea of sexual insurrection. Let us deal with this question as a whole. Why, after Mr. Chambers has succeeded at his one single point to-night, are we to have to begin afresh at other points to-morrow? We have established, I hope, that no man may presume to call Bottles profligate for marrying either his sister-in-law Hannah, or his niece Mary Jane. But this is not enough. A complication, like the complications of Greek tragedy, suggests itself to my mind. You noticed

Mr. Job Bottles. You must have seen his gaze resting on Mary Jane. But what with his cigars, his claret, his camellias, and the state of the money-market, Mr. Job Bottles is not a marrying man just at this moment. His brother is; but his brother cannot last for ever. Job, on the other hand, is full of vigour and vitality. We have heard of the patience of Job; how natural, if his brother marries Mary Jane now, that Job, with his habits tempered, his view of life calmed, and the state of the money-market different, may wish, when she is a widow some five years hence, to marry her himself. And we have arrangements which make this illegal! At such arrangements I hurl, with scorn and disgust, the burning words of our great leader—Ecclesiastical rubbish!

I thank thee, Friend! for teaching me that word.

Why, I ask, is Mr. Job Bottles's liberty, his Christian liberty, as my reverend friend yonder would say, to be abridged in this manner? And why is Protestant Dissent to be diverted from its great task of abolishing State Churches for the purpose of removing obstacles to the sexual insurrection of our race? Why are its more devoted ministers to be driven to contract, in the interests of Christian liberty, illegal unions of this kind themselves, *pour encourager les autres?* Why is the earnest liberalism and nonconformity of Lancashire and Yorkshire to be agitated on this question by hope deferred? Why is it to be put incessantly to the inconvenience of going to be married in Germany or in the United States, that greater and better Britain

> Which gives us manners, freedom, virtue, power?

Why must ideas on this topic have to be incubated for years in that nest of spicery, as the divine Shakspeare says, the mind of Mr. T. Chambers, before they can rule the world? For my part, my resolve is formed. This great question shall henceforth be seriously taken up in Fleet Street. As a sop to those toothless old Cerberuses, the bishops, who impotently exhibit still the passions, as Nick's French friends say, of another age, we will accord the continuance of the prohibition which forbids a man to marry his grandmother. But in other directions there shall be freedom. Mr. Chambers's admirable bill for enabling a woman to marry her sister's husband will doubtless pass triumphantly through Committee to-night, amidst the cheers of the ladies' gallery. The Liberal party must supplement that bill by two others: one enabling people to marry their brothers' and sisters' children, the other enabling a man to marry his brother's wife.'

But this glorious prospect fills me with an *afflatus* which can find its fit employment only in Fleet Street, and I am forced to subscribe myself,

Yours in haste,

A YOUNG LION.

(After our meeting at Laburnum House,—have I ever mentioned that the mansion of Mr. Bottles at Reigate is called Laburnum House?—intercourse was renewed between Arminius and me, but alas! not the close intimacy of old days. Perhaps, had I foreseen his approaching end, I should have made more strenuous efforts to regain his confidence. But it was not to be; and the following letter will show the cruel injustice with which Arminius, misled, I am sure, by Mr. Frederic Harrison and the party with whom that gentleman generally acts, could bring himself to speak of the man who has done so much to popularise his name and ideas.)

LETTER IX.

Arminius, starting for the Continent to take part in the War between France and Prussia, addresses a Disrespectful Farewell to Our People and Institutions.

SIR,— *Chequer Alley*,[1] *August* 9, 1870.

I AM off to-night for the Continent to join the Prussian army; if it had not been for an accidental circumstance with which I need not trouble you,[2] I should have been off a fortnight ago. I have no love for the preaching old drill-sergeant who is called King of Prussia, or for the audacious conspirator who pulls his wires; this conspirator and his rival conspirator, Louis Bonaparte, stand in my affections pretty much on a par. Both play their own game, and are obstacles to better things. I am a republican, I desire a republic for every country in Europe. I believe no

[1] After our rupture, Arminius removed from my immediate neighbourhood in Grub Street and established himself in Chequer Alley. I love to think that pilgrims will one day seek out his lodging there!—ED.

[2] His debts, alas!—ED.

country of Europe is so fitted to be a republic as Germany; I believe her difficulties are from her Hohenzollerns and Hapsburgs, and nothing else. I believe she will end by getting rid of these gentry; and that till that time comes the world will never know of what real greatness she is capable. But the present war, though we are led by the old drill-sergeant and his wire-puller, is a war of Germany against France. I must go and take part in it.

Before I go, I am moved to send you a few farewell remarks on your country and its position, about which you seem (and I am sure I do not wonder at it) to be much concerned and embarrassed just now. I have a great esteem for your nation, its genius, and its past history; and your present stage of development has been a subject of constant study and thought with me during the years I have lived here. Formerly I have more than once communicated my ideas to you, as occasion arose, through Mr. Matthew Arnold. But experience has shown me that, though willing and inquisitive, he has hardly brain enough for my purpose; besides, he has of late been plunged over head and ears in some dispute of Greeks of the Lower Empire with your foolish and impracticable Dissenters.[1]

[1] I make no comment on the tone and spirit of this; but I cannot forbear remarking that with the removal of Arminius and his influence

Finding him unserviceable, therefore, I address you myself; but I shall use some of the phrases with which he has familiarised you, because they save circumlocution; and as he learnt them all from me in the first instance, I see no reason why I should not take back my own property when I want it.

You are horrified and astounded at this war; horrified and astounded at the projects for altering the face of Europe which have been going on under your nose without your knowledge; horrified and astounded at the coolness with which foreign nations seem to leave you out of their account, or to estimate the chances and character of your intervention. They put you aside as if you were of no consequence; and this to you, who won the last great European war, and made the treaties of Vienna! The time, you think, has clearly come when you must make a demonstration. Your popular veteran, Lord Russell, declares amid universal applause that 'it is only the doubt that has long prevailed as to the course which England would take, which has encouraged and fostered all these projects of treaty, these combinations and intrigues.' You have but to speak plainly, and all will be well. Your great organ, the *Times*, not satisfied with itself conveying to

the main obstacle to my reconciliation with the Dissenters is withdrawn.—ED.

other Powers in the most magnificent manner (a duty, to say the truth, it always fulfils) 'what England believes to be due from and to her,' keeps exhorting your Government to do the same, to speak some brave words, and to speak them 'with promptitude and energy.'

I suppose your Government will do so. But forgive me if I tell you that to us disrespectful foreigners it makes very little difference in our estimate of you and of the future whether your Government does so or not. What gives the sense and significance to a Government's declarations is the power which is behind the Government. And what is the power which is behind the Government of England at the present epoch? The Philistines.

Simply and solely the Philistines, my dear friend, take my word for it! No, you will say, it is the nation. Pardon me, you have no nation. France is fused into one nation by the military spirit, and by her democracy, the great legacy of 1789, and subsisting even amidst her present corruption. Germany is fused into one nation by her idea of union and of the elevation of her whole people through culture. You are made up, as I have often told you through my poor disciple whom you so well know, of three distinct and unfused bodies,—Barbarians, Philistines, Populace. You call them aristocracy, middle, and lower class. One of these three must be predominant and lead.

Your lower class counts as yet for little or nothing. There is among them a small body of workmen with modern ideas, ideas of organisation, who may be a nucleus for the future; there are more of them Philistines in a small way, Philistines in embryo; but most of them are mere populace, or, to use your own kindly term, ***residuum.*** Such a class does not lead. Formerly your aristocracy led; it commanded the politics of the country; it had an aristocracy's ideas,—limited enough, but the idea of the country's grandeur and dignity was among them;—it took your middle and lower class along with it, and used them in its own way, and it made the great war which the battle of Waterloo crowned. But countries must outgrow a feudal organisation, and the political command of an aristocracy; your country has outgrown it. Your aristocracy tells upon England socially; by all the power of example of a class high-placed, rich, idle, self-indulgent, without mental life, it teaches your Philistines how to live fast. But it no longer rules; at most it but administers; the Philistines rule. That makes the difference between Lord Grenville and Lord Granville. When Lord Grenville had to speak to Europe in 1793, he had behind him your aristocracy, not indeed fused with your middle and lower class, but wielding them and using their force; and all the world knew what your aristocracy meant, for they knew it themselves. But Lord Granville has behind him, when he speaks to Europe in 1870, your Philistines or middle class; and how should the world know, or much care, what your middle class mean? for they do not know it themselves.

You may be mortified, but such is the truth. To be consequent and powerful, men must be bottomed on some vital idea or sentiment, which lends strength and certainty to their action. Your aristocracy of seventy years ago had the sentiment of the greatness of the old aristocratical England, and that sentiment gave them force to endure labours, anxiety, danger, disappointment, loss, restrictions of liberty. Your ruling middle class has no such foundation; hence its imbecility. It would tell you it believes in industrial development and liberty. Examine what it means by these, and you find it means getting rich and not being meddled with. And these it imagines to be self-acting powers for good, and agents of greatness; so that if more trade is done in England than anywhere else, if your personal independence is without a check, and your newspaper publicity unbounded, your Philistines think they are by the nature of things great, powerful, and admirable, and that their England has only to speak 'with promptitude and energy' in order to prevail.

My dear friend, do not hold your notions in this mechanical fashion, and do not be misled by that magnificent *Times* of yours; it is not the failing to speak 'with promptitude and energy' which injures you, it is the having nothing wise or consistent to say. Your ruling middle class have no great, seriously and truly conceived end;—therefore no greatness of soul or mind;—therefore no stedfastness and power in great affairs. While you are thus, in great affairs you do and must fumble. You imagine that your words must have weight with us because you are very rich and have unbounded liberty and publicity; you will find yourselves mistaken, and you will be bewildered. Then you may get involved in war, and you imagine that you cannot but make war well by dint of being so very rich; that you will just add a penny or two to your income-tax, change none of your ways, have clap-trap everywhere, as at present, unrestricted independence, legions of newspaper correspondents, boundless publicity; and thus, at a grand high pressure of expenditure, bustle, and excitement, arrive at a happy and triumphant result. But authority and victory over people who are in earnest means being in earnest oneself, and your Philistines are not in earnest; they have no idea great enough to make them so. They want to be important and authoritative; they want to enforce peace and curb the ambitious; they want to drive a roaring trade; they want to know and criticise all that is being done; they want no restrictions on their personal liberty, no interference with their usual way of going on; they want all these incompatible things equally and at once, because they have no idea deep and strong enough to subordinate everything else to itself. A correspondent of your own *Times* wrote from Berlin the other day, 'The complete control of this people by the State is most striking.' How would your Philistines like that? Not at all. But it is by sacrifices of this kind that success in great affairs is achieved; and when your Philistines find this out, or find that a raised income-tax, torrents of clap-trap, everybody saying what he likes and doing what he likes, newspaper correspondents everywhere, and a generally animated state of the public mind, are not enough to command success, they will be still more bewildered.

And this is the power which Lord Granville has behind him, and which is to give the force and meaning to his words. Poor Lord Granville! I imagine he is under no illusions. He knows the British Philistine, with his likes and dislikes, his effusion and confusion, his hot and cold fits, his want of dignity and of the stedfastness which comes from dignity, his want of ideas and of the stedfastness which comes from ideas;—he has seen him at work already. He has seen the Russian war and the Russian peace; a war and peace your aristocracy did not make and never would have made,—the British Philistine and his newspapers have the whole merit of it. In your social gatherings I know you have the habit of assuring one another that in some mysterious way the Russian war did you good in the eyes of Europe. Undeceive yourselves ; it did you nothing but harm, and Lord Granville is far too clever a man not to know it. Then, in the Denmark quarrel, your Philistines did not make war, indeed, but they threatened it. Surely in the Denmark case there was no want of brave words ; no failure to speak out 'with promptitude and energy.' And we all know what came of it. Unique British Philistine ! Is he most to be revered when he makes his wars or when he threatens them ? And at the prompting of this great backer Lord Granville is now to speak ! Probably he will have, as the French say, to execute him self ; only do not suppose that we are under any delusion as to the sort of force he has behind him.

My dear friend, I think I am perhaps writing to you for the last time, and by the love I bear to the England of your past literature and history, I do exhort your Philistine middle class, which is now England, to get, as I say, 'Geist ;' to search and not rest till it sees things more as they really are, and how little of a power over things as they really are is its money-making, or its unrestricted independence, or its newspaper publicity, or its Dissent, or any of the things with which it is now most taken; and how its newspapers deceive it when they tell it night and day that, being what it is, and having the objects it has, it commands the envy and deference of the world, and is on the sure road to greatness and happiness, if indeed it be not already arrived there. My dear friend, I have told you our German programme,—*the elevation of a whole people through culture.* That need not be your English programme, but surely you may have some better programme than this your present one,—*the beatification of a whole people through clap-trap.*

And now, my dear friend, it is time for me to go, and to what fate I go I know not; but this I know, that your country, where I have lived so long and seen so much, is on its way either to a great transformation or to a great disaster.

Your sincere well-wisher,

VON THUNDER-TEN-TRONCKH.

To

The EDITOR *of the* PALL MALL GAZETTE.

LETTER X.

Arminius, writing from the German Camp before Paris, comments, in his old Unappreciative Spirit, on the Attitude of Our Beloved Country in the Black Sea Question.

SIR,— *Before Paris, November* 21, 1870.

ANOTHER call 'to speak with promptitude and energy!' We had all been full of the Russian note, and here is your magnificent *Times* to tell me what the great heart of my dear English friends is thinking of it. You have not forgotten, of course, that sentence of Mr. Lowe (a descendant of Pangloss, and a sort of hereditary connexion of my family, though he took scant notice of me when I was in England): 'The destiny of England is in the great heart of England.' So, having a sincere regard for you, I always listen when your great heart speaks, that I may see what sort of a destiny it is about to create for you. And I find that it is now speaking very loud indeed, even louder than when I wrote to you in August last, and that it is bent on telling Russia 'with promptitude and energy,' in your own fine, full-mouthed fashion, 'what England believes to be due from and to her.' But even at such a crisis you do not forget to improve the occasion, and to indulge in the peculiar strain of moral reflection whence you get, your oracles tell us, 'that moral weight which your action, if conducted with tolerable judgment, is sure to command' (see, in the last *Edinburgh Review*, 'Germany, France, and England,' p. 591). It is not so much the matter of the Russian incident as its manner that pains you. 'We protest,' says your magnificent *Times*, 'that our sharpest feeling at the moment is pain at the apparent faithlessness of the Czar, and at the rudeness with which he has denounced the treaty.'

My dear friend, the weather is abominable, and the supply of tobacco, to me at any rate, short and bad; but I cannot resist sitting down without a pipe, in the mud, to write to you, when I see your great heart beating in this manner.

How like you,—how like the British Philistine in one of his hot fits, when he is moved to speak to Europe 'with promptitude and energy!' Of history, the future, the inevitable drive of events, not an inkling! A moral criticism of Russia and a wounded self-consequence,—that is all you are full of. The British Philistine all over!

At your present stage of development, as I have often remarked to you, this beneficent being is the depositary of your force, the mover of your policy. Your Government is, in and by itself, nothing. You are a self-governing people, you are represented by your 'strong middle part,' your Philistine: and this is what your Government must watch; this is what it must take its cue from.

Here, then, is your situation, that your Government does not and cannot really govern, but at present is and must be the mouthpiece of your Philistines; and that foreign Governments know this very well, know it to their cost. Nothing the best of them would like better than to deal with England seriously and respectfully,—the England of their traditions, the England of history; nothing, even, they would like better than to deal with the English Government,—as at any time it may happen to stand, composed of a dozen men more or less eminent,—seriously and respectfully. But, good God! it is not with these dozen men in their natural state that a foreign Government finds it has to deal; it is with these dozen men sitting in devout expectation to see how the cat will jump,—and that cat the British Philistine!

What statesman can deal seriously and respectfully when he finds that he is not dealing mind to mind with an intelligent equal, but that he is dealing with a tumult of likes and dislikes, hopes, panics, intrigues, stock-jobbing, quidnuncs, newspapers,—dealing with *ignorance* in short, for that one word contains it all,—behind his intelligent equal? Whatever he says to a British Minister, however convincing he may be, a foreign statesman knows that he has only half his hearer's attention, that only one of the British Minister's eyes is turned his way; the other eye is turned anxiously back on the home Philistines and the home press, and according as these finally go the British Minister must go too. This sort of thing demoralises your Ministers themselves in the end, even your able and honest ones, and makes them impossible to deal with. God forgive me if I do him wrong!—but I always suspect that your sly old Sir Hamilton Seymour, in his conversations with the Emperor Nicholas before the Crimean war, had at last your Philistines and your press, and their unmistakable bent, in his eye, and did not lead the poor Czar quite straight. If ever there was a man who respected England, and would have gone cordially and easily with a capable British minister, that man was Nicholas. England, Russia, and Austria are the Powers with a real interest in the Eastern question, and it ought to be settled fairly between them. Nicholas wished nothing better. Even if you would not thus settle the question, he would have forborne to any extent sooner than go to war with you, if he could only have known what you were really at. To be sure, as you did not know this yourselves, you could not possibly tell *him*, poor man! Louis Napoleon, meanwhile, had his prestige to make. France pulled the wires right and left; your Philistines had a passion for that old acrobat Lord Palmerston, who, clever as he was, had an aristocrat's inaptitude for ideas, and believed in upholding and renovating the Grand Turk; Lord Aberdeen knew better, but his eye was nervously fixed on the British Philistine and the British press. The British Philistine learnt that he was being treated with rudeness and must make his voice heard 'with promptitude and energy.' There was the usual explosion of passions, prejudices, stock-jobbing, newspaper-articles, chatter, and general ignorance, and the Czar found he must either submit to have capital made out of him by French vanity and Bonapartist necessities, or enter into the Crimean war. He entered into the Crimean war, and it broke his heart. France came out of the Crimean war the first Power in Europe, with French vanity and Bonapartist necessities fully served. You came out of it with the British Philistine's *rôle* in European affairs for the first time thoroughly recognised and appreciated.

Now for the 'faithlessness' and 'rudeness' of Russia's present proceeding. It has been known for the last half-dozen years in every chancery of Europe that Russia declared her position in the Black Sea to be intolerable, and was resolved to get it altered. France and Bonaparte, driven by the French *fat* as you are driven by the British Philistine,—and the French *fat* has proved a yet more fatal driver than yours, being debauched and immoral, as well as ignorant,—came to grief. I suppose Russia was not bound to wait till they were in a position to make capital out of her again. 'But with us, at any rate,' you will say, 'she might have dealt seriously and respectfully, instead of being faithless and rude.' Again, I believe Russia would have wished nothing better than to deal seriously with you, and to settle with you, not only the question of the Black Sea, but the whole Eastern question, which begins to press for settlement;—but it was impossible. It was impossible, because you offer nobody with whom a serious statesman can deal seriously. You offer a Government, with men in it eminent and able no doubt, but they do not make your policy; and their eye is always turning back to the power behind them which *does* make it. That power is the British Philistine. Was Russia, at a critical moment, to lose precious time waiting for the chance medley of accidents, intrigues, hot and cold fits, stock-jobbing, newspaper-articles, conversations on the railway, conversations on the omnibus, out of which grows the foreign policy of a self-governing people, when that self is the British Philistine? Russia thought not, and passed on to its object.

For my part, I cannot call this faithless, though I admit it may be called rude. But it was a rudeness which Governments with a serious object before them cannot well help committing when they are dealing with you. The question is: Will you at all better yourselves by having now one of your hot fits, speaking 'with promptitude and energy,' and, in fact, going to war with Russia for what she has done? Alas, my dear friend, this would be throwing the handle after the blade with a vengeance! Because your governing part, your Philistine middle class, is ignorant and impracticable, Russia has unceremoniously taken a step in the Eastern question without you. And what does your going to war with Russia in the present posture of affairs mean? It means backing up the Porte to show fight; going in, in Lord Palmerston's old line, for upholding and renovating the Grand Turk;—it means fighting against nature. This is how the ignorant and impracticable get punished; they are made to smart for being ignorant and impracticable, and they can only resent being made to smart by showing themselves more ignorant and impracticable still. Do not do so, my dear friend! Russia has no wish to quarrel with you; she had a serious object to gain, and, as time pressed, she did what she had to do without entering into an interminable and possibly fruitless conversation with your 'young man from the country.' But she does not mean more than her avowed object, which was really indispensable to her; she will try to make things now as pleasant as she can (consistently with getting her object) for your young man from the country; and the moment the young man has clear ideas she will ask nothing better than to deal with him seriously and respectfully.

All turns upon that, my dear friend!—the improving your young man and giving him clear ideas. At present he is vulgar, ignorant, and consequential; and because he is vulgar, he is ignoble; because he is ignorant, he is unstable; because he is consequential, he is on the look-out for affronts and apt to fly into a heat. With these qualities he cannot but bring mortifications upon you and himself, so long as he governs or tries to govern. All nations have their young man of this sort, but with you alone he governs, and hence the European importance of him and his failings. You know how I dislike the Junkerism and militarism of my own Prussian country and its government; all I say is, that the self-government of your Philistine is as bad, or even worse. There is nothing like it anywhere; for America, which in some respects resembles you, has not your necessary relations with Europe; and, besides, her Philistines, if they govern, administer also, and get the training which great affairs give. With you the Barbarians administer, the Philistines govern; between them your policy is made. One class contributes its want of ideas, the other its want of dignity;—an unlucky mixture for you, my dear friend, it must be confessed!

The worst of it is, I do not see how things are to get better with you at present. The Philistines rule and rule abominably, but for the moment there is no remedy. Bismarck would say, 'Muzzle them;' but I know well this cannot, nay, should not be. I say, 'Improve them;' but for this time is needed. Your Government might, no doubt, do something to speed the improvement, if it cared a little more, in serving the Philistines, for what might do them good, and a little less for what might please them; but perhaps this is too much to expect from your Government. So you must needs have, my dear friend, I am afraid, what these poor wretched people here call a *mauvais quart d'heure*, in which you will be peculiarly liable to mistakes, mortifications, and troubles. While this period lasts, *your strength*, forgive me for saying so, *is to sit still.* What your friends (of whom I am one) must wish for you is that you may keep as quiet as possible; that the British Philistine may not be moved much to speak to Europe 'with promptitude and energy;' that he may get out of his hot fits always as soon as possible. And perhaps you *are* getting out of your recent hot fit already ; perhaps, even while I write, you have got into one of your cold fits, and are all for pacific solutions and moral suasion. I say, Heaven grant it ! with all my heart.

And, meanwhile, how are my friends in England? I think I see Bottles by the Royal Exchange at this moment, holding forth, with the *Times* in his hand, on 'the perfect unanimity of opinion among the mercantile community of the City of London !' I think I hear poor Mr. Matthew Arnold's platitudes about 'the two great conquests of English energy,—*liberty and publicity !*' Liberty, my dear friend, to make fools of yourselves, and publicity to tell all the world you are doing so.

Forgive my *ur-deutsch* frankness, and believe me, your sincere friend,

VON THUNDER-TEN-TRONCKH.

To

The EDITOR *of the* PALL MALL GAZETTE.

LETTER XI.

I take up the Cudgels for Our Beloved Country.

SIR,— *Grub Street, November 25, 1870.*

I KNOW by experience how hard it is to get my bald, disjointed chat, as Arminius calls it, into the newspapers in these stirring times, and that was why I did not attempt to complain of that extraordinary effusion of his which you published in August last. He must have written that letter, with its unhandsome remarks at my expense, just after I had parted with him at his lodgings in Chequer Alley, with expressions of the tenderest concern, before he went off to the war. Since then, I have discovered that he had referred nearly all his tradespeople to me for payment ; I am daily besieged in my garret by his tobacconist, and when I get out, the street is made quite intolerable to me by the violence of his washerwoman, though I am sure Arminius, like all foreigners, always gave his washerwoman as little trouble as possible. These things have nettled me a good deal ; and now there comes this new letter of his from Paris, in which, besides totally uncalled-for sneers at Mr. Bottles and me, Arminius indulges in an outrageous attack on my country and her behaviour in this Russian business. I have kept silence for a few days to make sure of being perfectly cool; but now, Sir, I do hope you will give me space for a few lines in reply to him.

About the Russian note I disagree with Arminius *in toto.* I go thoroughly along with Lord Shaftesbury, whose admirable letter to the *Times* proves, what I have always thought, how unjust Arminius is in denying ideas to the British aristocracy. A treaty is a promise,—so I read Lord Shaftesbury's argument; men should keep their promises; if bad men will not, good men must compel them.

It is singular, Sir, but in my immediate neighbourhood here in Cripplegate we have lately had a case which exactly illustrates the Russian difficulty, and bears out Lord Shaftesbury's argument. We all do our marketing in Whitecross Street; and in Whitecross Street is a famous tripe-shop which I always visit before entertaining Arminius, who, like all North Germans, and like our own celebrated Dr. Johnson, is a very gross feeder. Two powerful labourers, who lodge like Arminius in Chequer Alley, and who never could abide one another, used to meet at this tripe-shop and quarrel till it became manifest that the shop could not stand two such customers together, and that one of the couple must give up going there. The fellows' names were Mike and Dennis; it was generally thought the chief blame in the quarrel lay with Mike, who was at any rate much the less plausible man of the two, besides being greatly the bigger. However that may be, the excellent City Missionary in this quarter, the Rev. *J-hn B-ll* (I forbear to write his name at length for fear of bringing a blush to his worthy cheek), took Dennis's part in the matter. He and Dennis set both together upon Mike, and got the best of him. It was Dennis who appeared to do the most in the set-to; at all events, he got the whole credit, although I have heard the Rev. *J-hn B-ll* (who was undoubtedly a formidable fellow in his old unregenerate days) describe at tea in the Mission Room how he got his stick between Mike's legs at all the critical moments; how he felt fresher and stronger when the fight ended than when it began; and how his behaviour had somehow the effect of leaving on the bystanders' minds an impression immensely to his advantage. What is quite certain is, that not only did our reverend friend take part in the engagement, but that also, before, during, and after the struggle, his exhortations and admonitions to Mike, Dennis, the bystanders, and himself, never ceased, and were most edifying. Mike finally, as I said, had to give in, and he was obliged to make a solemn promise to Dennis and the City Missionary that he would use the tripe-shop no more. On this condition a treaty was patched up, and peace reigned in Cripplegate.

And now, Sir, comes the startling point of resemblance to the present Russian difficulty. A great big hulking German, called Fritz, has been for some time taking a lead in our neighbourhood, and carrying his head a great deal higher in Whitecross Street Market than Dennis liked. At last Dennis could stand it no longer; he picked a quarrel with Fritz, and they had a battle-royal to prove which was master. In this encounter our City Missionary took no part, though he bestowed, as usual, on both sides good advice and beautiful sentiments in abundance. Dennis had no luck this time; he got horribly belaboured, and now lies confined to his bed at his lodgings, almost past praying for. But what do you think has been Mike's conduct at this juncture? Seeing Dennis disabled, he addressed to the City Missionary an indecent scrawl, couched in language with which I will not sully your pages, to the effect that the tripe-shop lay handy to his door (which is true enough); and that use it he needs must, and use it he would, in spite of all the Rev. *J-hn B-ll* might say or do to stop him.

The feelings, Sir, of the worthy Missionary at this communication may be easier imagined than described. He launched at Mike the most indignant moral rebuke; the brute put his thumb to his nose. To get Mike out of the tripe-shop there is nothing left but physical force. Yet how is our estimable friend to proceed? Years of outpouring, since he has been engaged in mission-work, have somewhat damaged his wind; the hospitalities of the more serious-minded citizens of Cripplegate to a man in his position have been, I hope, what they should be; there are apprehensions, if violent exercise is taken, of gout in the stomach. Dennis can do nothing; what is worse, Fritz has been seen to wink his eye at Mike in a way to beget grave suspicion that the ruffians have a secret compact together. The general feeling in Cripplegate is that nothing much can be done, and that Mike must be allowed to resort again to the tripe-shop.

But I ask you, Sir, is this morally defensible? Is it right? Is it honest? Has not Lord Shaftesbury's English heart (if it is not presumptuous in me to speak thus of a person in his lordship's position) guided him true in the precisely similar case of Russia? A treaty is a promise, and we have a moral right to demand that promises shall be kept. If Mike wanted to use the tripe-shop, he should have waited till Dennis was about again and could talk things over with the City Missionary, and then, perhaps, the two might have been found willing to absolve Mike from his promise. His present conduct is inexcusable; the only comfort is that the Rev. *J-hn B-ll* has a faithful press still to back him, and that Mike is being subjected to a fearful daily castigation in the columns of the *Band of Hope Review.*

Therefore, Sir, as to Russia I emphatically think Arminius wrong. His sneers at my zeal for the grand principles of liberty and publicity I have hardly left myself space to notice. But, Sir, I do believe, with Mr. Bright, that the great function committed by Providence to our English-speaking race is 'the assertion of personal liberty.' If this be an error, I would rather, I own, err with Mr. Bright than be right with Von Thunder-ten-Tronckh. I know Von T. maintains that we so intently pursue liberty and publicity as quite to neglect wisdom and virtue; for which alone, he says, liberty and publicity are worth having. But I will ask him, Sir, have we ever given liberty and publicity a full trial? Take liberty. The Lord Chancellor has, indeed, provided for Mr. Beales, and it is whispered that Colonel Dickson will have a high command in the approaching Russian war;—*but why is Mr. Bradlaugh not yet a Dean?* These, Sir, are the omissions, these the failures to carry into full effect our own great principles, which drive earnest Liberals to despair!

Again, take the principle of publicity. Arminius (who,

as an observer of manners, attended the proceedings in the Mordaunt case, and again in the Park and Boulton case, with unflagging assiduity) has said to me scores of times :—'By shooting all this garbage on your public, you are preparing and assuring for your English people an immorality as deep and wide as that which destroys the Latin nations.' What is my reply? That we have never yet given publicity a fair trial. It is true, when a member of Parliament wanted to abridge the publicity given to the Mordaunt case, the Government earnestly reminded him that it had been the solemn decision of the House of Commons that all the proceedings of the Divorce Court should be open as the day. It is true, when there was a suggestion to hear the Boulton and Park case in private, the upright magistrate who was appealed to said firmly that he could never trifle with the public mind in that manner. All this was as it should be; so far, so good. But was the publicity thus secured for these cases perfectly full and entire? Were there not some places which the details did not reach? There were few, but there were some. And this while the Government has an organ of its own, the *London Gazette*, dull, high-priced, and of comparatively limited circulation. I say, make the price of the *London Gazette* a halfpenny; change its name to the *London Gazette and Divorce Intelligencer*; let it include, besides divorce news, all cases whatever that have an interest of the same nature for the public mind; distribute it *gratis* to mechanics' institutes, workmen's halls, seminaries for the young (these latter more especially);—and then you will be giving the principle of publicity a full trial. This is what I often say to Arminius; and, when he looks astounded, I reassure him with a sentence which, I know very well, the moment I make it public, will be stolen by all the Liberal newspapers. But it is getting near Christmas-time, and I do not mind making them a present of it. It is this:—*The spear of freedom, like that of Achilles, has the power to heal the wounds which itself makes!*

This Arminius can never answer; and, badly as he has treated me, my heart relents to think of the stupefied face I have often seen him with at hearing it. Poor Arminius! I wonder what he is doing now? If the Prussians keep sticking in the mud before Paris, how will he continue to bear the wet weather, the winter nights, the exposure? And may not his prolonged requisitions for tobacco and sausages (merciless I know they will be!) prove too much at last for the patience of even some down-trodden worm of a French *bourgeois*? Or, again, this is the hour for a *sortie*, and Arminius is as brave as a lion. I go to my garret-window; it is just midnight; how gloomy is Grub Street at this hour! I look towards the familiar regions of Whitecross Street Market and Chequer Alley; the venerable pile of Cripplegate Church, which I could never get Arminius to enter, rises darkly and sadly before me. Dismal presentiments begin to crowd upon my soul, and I sign myself,

Sir, your uneasy servant,

MATTHEW ARNOLD.

To

The EDITOR *of the* PALL MALL GAZETTE.

LETTER XII.

'*Life*,' *as Mr. G. A. Sala says*, '*a Dream!*'

Mon Cher,— *Versailles, November* 26, 1870.

An event has just happened which I confess frankly will afflict others more than it does me, but which you ought to be informed of.

Early this morning I was passing between Rueil and Bougival, opposite Mont Valérien. How came I in that place at that hour? *Mon cher*, forgive my folly! You have read *Romeo and Juliet*, you have seen me at Cremorne, and though Mars has just now this *belle France* in his gripe, yet you remember, I hope, enough of your classics to know that, where Mars is, Venus is never very far off. Early this morning, then, I was between Rueil and Bougival, with Mont Valérien in grim proximity. On a bank by a poplar-tree at the roadside I saw a knot of German soldiers, gathered evidently round a wounded man. I approached and frankly tendered my help, in the name of British humanity. What answer I may have got

I do not know; for, petrified with astonishment, I recognised in the wounded man our familiar acquaintance, Arminius von Thunder-ten-Tronckh. A Prussian helmet was stuck on his head, but there was the old hassock of whity-brown hair,—there was the old square face,—there was the old blue pilot coat! He was shot through the chest, and evidently near his end. He had been on outpost duty;—the night had been quiet, but a few random shots had been fired. One of these had struck Arminius in the breast, and gone right through his body. By this stray bullet, without glory, without a battle, without even a foe in sight, had fallen the last of the Von Thunder-ten-Tronckhs!

He knew me, and with a nod, 'Ah,' said he, 'the rowdy Philistine!' You know his turn, *outré* in my opinion, for flinging nicknames right and left. The present, however, was not a moment for resentment. The Germans saw that their comrade was in friendly hands, and gladly left him with me. He had evidently but a few minutes to live. I sate down on the bank by him, and asked him if I could do anything to relieve him. He shook his head. Any message to his friends in England? He nodded. I ran over the most prominent names which occurred to me of the old set. First, our Amphitryon, Mr. Bottles. 'Say to Bottles from me,' said Arminius coldly, 'that I hope he will be comfortable with his dead wife's sister.' Next, Mr. Frederic Harrison. 'Tell him,' says Arminius, 'to do more in literature,—he has a talent for it; and to avoid Carlylese as he would the devil.' Then I mentioned a personage to whom Arminius had taken a great fancy last spring, and of whose witty writings some people had, absurdly enough, given Mr. Matthew Arnold the credit,—Azamat-Batuk. Both writers are simple; but Azamat's is the simplicity of shrewdness, the other's of helplessness. At hearing the clever Turk's name, 'Tell him only,' whispers Arminius, 'when he writes about the sex, not to show such a turn for sailing so very near the wind!' Lastly, I mentioned Mr. Matthew Arnold. I hope I rate this poor soul's feeble and rambling performances at their proper value; but I am bound to say that at the mention of his name Arminius showed signs of tenderness. 'Poor fellow!' sighed he; 'he had a soft head, but I valued his heart. Tell him I leave him my ideas,—the easier ones; and advise him from me,' he added, with a faint smile, 'to let his Dissenters go to the devil their own way!'

At this instant there was a movement on the road at a little distance from where we were,—some of the Prussian Princes, I believe, passing; at any rate, we heard the honest German soldiers *Hoch-ing*, hurrahing, and God-blessing, in their true-hearted but somewhat *rococo* manner. A flush passed over Von Thunder-ten-Tronckh's face. 'God bless *Germany*,' he murmured, 'and confound all her kings and princelings!' These were his last coherent words. His eyes closed and he seemed to become unconscious. I stooped over him and inquired if he had any wishes about his interment. 'Pangloss—Mr. Lowe—mausoleum—Caterham,' was all that, in broken words, I could gather from him. His breath came with more and more difficulty, his fingers felt instinctively for his tobacco-pouch, his lips twitched;—he was gone.

So died, *mon cher*, an arrant Republican, and, to speak my real mind, a most unpleasant companion. His great name and lineage imposed on the Bottles family, and authors who had never succeeded with the British public took pleasure in his disparaging criticisms on our free and noble country; but for my part I always thought him an overrated man.

Meanwhile I was alone with his remains. His notion of their being transported to Caterham was of course impracticable. Still, I did not like to leave an old acquaintance to the crows, and I looked round in perplexity. Fortune in the most unexpected manner befriended me. The grounds of a handsome villa came down to the road close to where I was; at the end of the grounds and overhanging the road was a summer-house. Its shutters had been closed when I first discovered Arminius; but while I was occupied with him they had been opened, and a gay trio was visible within the summer-house at breakfast. I could scarcely believe my eyes for satisfaction. Three English members of Parliament, celebrated for their ardent charity and advanced Liberalism, were sitting before me adorned with a red cross and eating a Strasburg pie! I approached them and requested their aid to bury Arminius. My request seemed to occasion them painful embarrassment; they muttered something about 'a breach of the understanding,' and went on with their breakfast. I insisted, however; and at length, having stipulated that what they were about to do should on no account be drawn into a precedent, they left their breakfast, and together we buried Arminius under the poplar-tree. It was a hurried business, for my friends had an engagement to lunch at Versailles at noon. Poor Von Thunder-ten-Tronckh, the earth lies light on him, indeed! I could see, as I left him, the blue of his pilot-coat and the whity-brown of his hair through the mould we had scattered over him.

My benevolent helpers and I then made our way together to Versailles. As I parted from them at the Hôtel des Reservoirs I met Sala. Little as I liked Arminius, the melancholy scene I had just gone through had shaken me, and I needed sympathy. I told Sala what had happened. 'The old story,' says Sala; '*life a dream!* Take a glass of brandy.' He then inquired who my friends were. 'Three admirable members of Parliament,' I cried, 'who, donning the cross of charity——' 'I know,' interrupted Sala; 'the cleverest thing out!'

But the emotions of this agitating day were not yet over. While Sala was speaking, a group had formed before the hotel near us, and our attention was drawn to its central figure. Dr. Russell, of the *Times*, was preparing to mount his war-horse. You know the sort of thing,—he has described it himself over and over again. Bismarck at his horse's head, the Crown Prince holding his stirrup, and the old King of Prussia hoisting Russell into the saddle. When he was there, the distinguished public servant waved his hand in acknowledgment, and rode slowly down the street, accompanied by the *gamins* of Versailles, who even in their present dejection could not forbear a few involuntary cries of '*Quel homme!*' Always unassuming, he alighted at the lodgings of the Grand Duke of Oldenburg, a potentate of the second or even the third order, who had beckoned to him from the window.

The agitation of this scene for me, however (may I not

add, *mon cher*, for you also, and for the whole British press?), lay in a suggestion which it called forth from Sala. 'It is all very well,' said Sala, 'but old Russell's guns are getting a little honeycombed; anybody can perceive that. He will have to be pensioned off, and why should not you succeed him?' We passed the afternoon in talking the thing over, and I think I may assure you that a train has been laid of which you will see the effects shortly.

For my part, I can afford to wait till the pear is ripe; yet I cannot, without a thrill of excitement, think of inoculating the respectable but somewhat ponderous *Times* and its readers with the divine madness of our new style,—the style we have formed upon Sala. The world, *mon cher*, knows that man but imperfectly. I do not class him with the great masters of human thought and human literature,—Plato, Shakspeare, Confucius, Charles Dickens. Sala, like us his disciples, has studied in the book of the world even more than in the world of books. But his career and genius have given him somehow the secret of a literary mixture novel and fascinating in the last degree: he blends the airy epicureanism of the *salons* of Augustus with the full-bodied gaiety of our English Cider-cellar. With our people and country, *mon cher*, this mixture, you may rely upon it, is now the very thing to go down; there arises every day a larger public for it ; and we, Sala's disciples, may be trusted not willingly to let it die.—*Tout à vous*,

A YOUNG LION.[1]

To

The EDITOR *of the* PALL MALL GAZETTE.

[1] I am bound to say that in attempting to verify Leo's graphic description of Dr. Russell's mounting on horseback, from the latter's own excellent correspondence, to which Leo refers us, I have been unsuccessful. Repeatedly I have seemed to be on the trace of what my friend meant, but the particular description he alludes to I have never been lucky enough to light upon.

I may add that, in spite of what Leo says of the train he and Mr. Sala have laid, of Dr. Russell's approaching retirement, of Leo's prospect of succeeding him, of the charm of the leonine style, and of the disposition of the public mind to be fascinated by it,—I cannot myself believe that either the public, or the proprietors of the *Times*, are yet ripe for a change so revolutionary. But Leo was always sanguine.—ED.

(I HAVE thought that the memorial raised to Arminius would not be complete without the following essay, in which, though his name is not actually mentioned, he will be at once recognised as the leading spirit of the foreigners whose conversation is quoted.

Much as I owe to his intellect, I cannot help sometimes regretting that the spirit of youthful paradox which led me originally to question the perfections of my countrymen, should have been, as it were, prevented from dying out by my meeting, six years ago, with Arminius. The *Saturday Review*, in an article called 'Mr. Matthew Arnold and his Countrymen,' had taken my correction in hand, and I was in a fair way of amendment, when the intervention of Arminius stopped the cure, and turned me, as has been often said, into a mere mouthpiece of this dogmatic young Prussian. It was not that I did not often dislike his spirit and boldly stand up to him ; but, on the whole, my intellect was (there is no use denying it) overmatched by his. The following essay, which appeared at the beginning of 1866, was the first proof of this fatal predominance, which has in many ways cost me so dear.)—ED.

III

My Countrymen.

About a year ago the *Saturday Review* published an article which gave me, as its articles often do give me, much food for reflection. The article was about the unjust estimate which, says the *Saturday Review*, I form of my countrymen, and about the indecency of talking of 'British Philistines.' It appears that I assume the truth of the transcendental system of philosophy,[1] and then lecture my wiser countrymen because they will not join me in recognising as eternal truths a set of platitudes which may be proved to be false. 'Now there is in England a school of philosophy which thoroughly understands, and, on theoretical grounds, deliberately rejects, the philosophical theory which Mr. Arnold accuses the English nation of neglecting; and the practical efforts of the English people, especially their practical efforts in the way of criticism, are for the most part strictly in accordance with the principles of that philosophy.'

[1] Philosophy has always been bringing me into trouble.—Ed.

I do not quite know what to say about the transcendental system of philosophy, for I am a mere dabbler in these great matters, and to grasp and hold a system of philosophy is a feat much beyond my strength; but I certainly did talk about British Philistines, and to call people Philistines when they are doing just what the wisest men in the country have settled to be quite right, does seem unreasonable, not to say indecent. Being really the most teachable man alive, I could not help making, after I had read the article in the *Saturday Review*, a serious return, as the French say, upon myself; and I resolved never to call my countrymen Philistines again till I had thought more about it, and could be quite sure I was not committing an indecency.

I was very much fortified in this good resolution by something else which happened about the same time. Every one knows that the heart of the English nation is its middle class; there had been a good deal of talk, a year ago, about the education of this class, and I, among others, had imagined it was not good, and that the middle class suffered by its not being better. But Mr. Bazley,[1] the member for Manchester, who is a kind of representative of this class, made a speech last year at Manchester, the middle-class metropolis, which shook me a good deal.

[1] Now Sir Thomas Bazley, Bart.—Ed.

'During the last few months,' said Mr. Bazley, 'there had been a cry that middle-class education ought to receive more attention. He confessed himself very much surprised by the clamour that was raised. He did not think that class need excite the sympathy either of the legislature or the public.' Much to the same effect spoke Mr. Miall, another middle-class leader, in the *Nonconformist*: 'Middle-class education seems to be the favourite topic of the hour, and we must confess to a feeling of shame at the nonsense which is being uttered on the subject. It might be thought from what is said, that this section of the community, which has done everything else so well,—which has astonished the world by its energy, enterprise, and self-reliance, which is continually striking out new paths of industry and subduing the forces of nature,—cannot, from some mysterious reason, get their children properly educated.' Still more strong were the words of the *Daily News* (I love to range all the evidence in black and white before me, though it tends to my own discomfiture) about the blunder some of us were making: 'All the world knows that the great middle class of this country supplies the mind, the will, and the power for all the great and good things that have to be done, and it is not likely that that class should surrender its powers and privileges in the one case of the training of its own children. How the idea of such a scheme can have occurred to anybody, how it can have been imagined that parents and schoolmasters in the most independent, and active, and enlightened class of English society,[1] how it can have been supposed that the class which has done all the great things that have been done in all departments, will beg the Government to send inspectors through its schools, when it can itself command whatever advantages exist, might seem unintelligible but for two or three considerations.' These considerations do not much matter just now; but it is clear how perfectly Mr. Bazley's stand was a stand such as it becomes a representative man like Mr. Bazley to make, and how well the *Daily Telegraph* might say of the speech: 'It was at once grand, genial, national, and distinct;' and the *Morning Star* of the speaker: 'He talked to his constituents as Manchester people like to be talked to, in the language of clear, manly intelligence, which penetrates through sophisms, ignores commonplaces, and gives to conventional illusions their true value. His speech was thoroughly instinct with that earnest good sense which characterises Manchester, and which, indeed, may be fairly

[1] How very fine and striking is this language! Eloquent as is the homage which our newspapers still pay in the same quarter, it seems as if, in 1866, their eulogy had a ring and fulness which it has since in some measure lost.—ED.

set down as the general characteristic of England and Englishmen everywhere.'

Of course if Philistinism is characteristic of the British nation just now, it must in a special way be characteristic of the representative part of the British nation, the part by which the British nation is what it is, and does all its best things, the middle class. And the newspapers, who have so many more means than I of knowing the truth, and who have that trenchant authoritative style for communicating it which makes so great an impression, say that the British middle class is characterised, not by Philistinism, but by enlightenment; by a passion for penetrating through sophisms, ignoring commonplaces, and giving to conventional illusions their true value. Evidently it is nonsense, as the *Daily News* says, to think that this great middle class which supplies the mind, the will, and the power for all the great and good things that have to be done, should want its schools, the nurseries of its admirable intelligence, meddled with. It may easily be imagined that all this, coming on the top of the *Saturday Review's* rebuke of me for indecency, was enough to set me meditating; and after a long and painful self-examination, I saw that I had been making a great mistake. Instead of confining myself to what alone I had any business with,—the slow and obscure work of trying to understand things, to see them as they are,—I had been meddling with practice, proposing this and that, saying how it might be if we established this or that. So I was suffering deservedly in being taunted with hawking about my nostrums of State schools for a class much too wise to want them, and of an Academy for people who have an inimitable style already. To be sure, I had said that schools ought to be things of local, not State, institution and management, and that we ought not to have an Academy; but that makes no difference. I saw what danger I had been running by thus intruding into a sphere where I have no business, and I resolved to offend in this way no more.

This I say as a sincere penitent; but I do not see that there is any harm in my still trying to know and understand things, if I keep humbly to that, and do not meddle with greater matters, which are out of my reach. So having once got into my head this notion of British Philistinism and of the want of clear and large intelligence in our middle class, I do not consider myself bound at once to put away and crush such a notion, as people are told to do with their religious doubts; nor, when the *Saturday Review* tells me that no nation in the world is so logical as the English nation, and the *Morning Star*, that our grand national characteristic is a clear intelligence which penetrates through sophisms, ignores commonplaces, and gives to conventional illusions their true value, do I feel myself compelled to receive these propositions with absolute submission as articles of faith, transcending reason ; indeed, this would be transcendentalism, which the *Saturday Review* condemns. Canvass them, then, as mere matters of speculation, I may ; and having lately had occasion to travel on the Continent for many months, during which I was thrown in company with a great variety of people, I remembered what Burns says of the profitableness of trying to see ourselves as others see us, and I kept on the watch for anything to confirm or contradict my old notion, in which, without absolutely giving it up, I had begun certainly to be much shaken and staggered.

I must say that the foreign opinion about us is not at all like that of the *Saturday Review* and the *Morning Star.* I know how madly the foreigners envy us, and that this must warp their judgment ; I know, too, that this test of foreign opinion can never be decisive ; I only take it for what it is worth, and as a contribution to our study of the matter in question. But I do really think that the admirers of our great middle class, which has, as its friends and enemies both agree, risen into such preponderating importance of late years, and now returns the House of Commons, dictates the policy of Ministers, makes the newspapers speak with its voice, and in short governs the country,—I do think, I say, the admirers of this great class would be astounded if they could hear how cavalierly a foreigner treats this country of their making and managing. 'It is not so much that we dislike England,' a Prussian official,[1] with the graceful tact of his nation, said to me the other day, 'as that we think little of her.' The *Cologne Gazette*, perhaps the chief newspaper of Germany, published in the summer a series of letters, much esteemed, I believe, by military men, on the armies of the leading Continental powers. The writer was a German officer, but not a Prussian. Speaking of the false military system followed by the Emperor Nicholas, whose great aim was to turn his soldiers into perfectly drilled machines, and contrasting this with the free play left to the individual soldier in the French system: 'In consequence of their purely mechanical training,' says this writer, 'the Russians, in spite of their splendid courage, were in the Crimean war constantly beaten by the French, nay, decidedly beaten *even by the English and the Turks*.'[2] Hardly a German newspaper can discuss territorial changes in Europe but it will add, after its remarks on the probable policy of France in this or that event: 'England will

[1] Not Arminius.—Ed.

[2] 'Ja, selbst von den Engländern und Türken entschieden geschlagen.'

probably make a fuss, but what England thinks is of no importance.' I believe the German newspapers must keep a phrase of that kind stereotyped, they use it so often. France is our very good friend just now, but at bottom our 'clear intelligence penetrating through sophisms,' and so on, is not held in much more esteem there than in Germany. One of the gravest and most moderate of French newspapers,—a newspaper, too, our very good friend, like France herself, into the bargain,—broke out lately, when some jealousy of the proposed Cholera Commission in the East was shown on this side the water, in terms which, though less rough than the 'great fool' of the *Saturday Review*, were still far from flattering. 'Let us speak to these English the only language they can comprehend. England lives for her trade; Cholera interrupts trade; therefore it is for England's interest to join in precautions against Cholera.'[1]

Compliments of this sort are displeasing to remember, displeasing to repeat; but their abundance strikes the attention; and then the happy unconsciousness of those at whom they are aimed, their state of imperturbable self-satisfaction, strikes the attention too, and makes an inquisitive mind quite eager to see its way clearly in this apparent

[1] Poor France! As Mr. Bottles says, neither her favourable nor her unfavourable criticisms are of much consequence just now.—ED.

game of cross purposes. For never, surely, was there such a game of cross purposes played. It came to its height when Lord Palmerston died the other day. Lord Palmerston was England; 'the best type of our age and country,' the *Times* well called him; he was 'a great representative man, emphatically the English Minister;' the interpreter of the wishes of that great middle class of this country which supplies the mind, the will, and the power requisite for all the great and good things that have to be done, and therefore 'acknowledged by a whole people as their best impersonation.' Monsieur Thiers says of Pitt, that though he used and abused the strength of England, she was the second country in the world at the time of his death, and the first eight years afterwards. That was after Waterloo and the triumphs of Wellington. And that era of primacy and triumphs, Lord Palmerston, say the English newspapers, has carried on to this hour. 'What Wellington was as a soldier, that was Palmerston as a statesman.' When I read these words in some foreign city or other, I could not help rubbing my eyes and asking myself if I was dreaming. Why, taking Lord Palmerston's career from 1830 (when he first became Foreign Secretary) to his death, there cannot be a shadow of doubt, for any one with eyes and ears in his head, that he found England the first Power in the world's estimation, and that he leaves her the third, after France[1] and the United States. I am no politician; I mean no disparagement at all to Lord Palmerston, to whose talents and qualities I hope I can do justice; and indeed it is not Lord Palmerston's policy, or any minister's policy, that is in question here, it is the policy of all of us, it is the policy of England; for in a government such as ours is at present, it is only, as we are are so often reminded, by interpreting public opinion, by being 'the best type of his age and country,' that a minister governs; and Lord Palmerston's greatness lay precisely in our all 'acknowledging him as our best impersonation.' Well, then, to this our logic, our practical efforts in the way of criticism, our clear manly intelligence penetrating through sophisms and ignoring commonplaces, and above all, our redoubtable phalanx possessing these advantages in the highest degree, our great middle class, which makes Parliament, and which supplies the mind, the will, and the power requisite for all the great and good things that have to be done, have brought us; to the third place in the world's estimation, instead of the first. He who disbelieves it, let him go round to every embassy in Europe and ask if it is not true.

The foreigners, indeed, are in no doubt as to the real authors of the policy of modern England; they know that

[1] Heu incredibiles humanarum rerum mutationes!—ED.

ours is no longer a policy of Pitts and aristocracies,[1] disposing of every movement of the hoodwinked nation to whom they dictate it; they know that our policy is now dictated by the strong middle part of England,—England happy, as Mr. Lowe, quoting Aristotle, says, in having her middle part strong and her extremes weak; and that, though we are administered by one of our weak extremes, the aristocracy, these managers administer us, as a weak extreme naturally must, with a nervous attention to the wishes of the strong middle part, whose agents they are. It was not the aristocracy which made the Crimean war; it was the strong middle part—the constituencies. It was the strong middle part which showered abuse and threats on Germany for mishandling Denmark; and when Germany gruffly answered, *Come and stop us*, slapped its pockets, and vowed that it had never had the slightest notion of pushing matters so far as this. It was the strong middle part which, by the voice of its favourite newspapers, kept threatening Germany, after she had snapped her fingers at us, with a future chastisement from France, just as a smarting schoolboy threatens his bully with a drubbing to come from some big boy in the background. It was the strong middle part, speaking through the same newspapers, which was full of coldness, slights, and sermons for the American Federals

[1] Arminius; he says it over again in his last letter but one.—ED.

during their late struggle; and as soon as they had succeeded, discovered that it had always wished them well, and that nothing was so much to be desired as that the United States, and we, should be the fastest friends possible. Some people will say that the aristocracy was an equal offender in this respect: very likely: but the behaviour of the strong middle part makes more impression than the behaviour of a weak extreme; and the more so, because from the middle class, their fellows in numberless ways, the Americans expected sympathy, while from the aristocracy they expected none. And, in general, the faults with which foreigners reproach us in the matters named,—rash engagement, intemperate threatening, undignified retreat, ill-timed cordiality,—are not the faults of an aristocracy, by nature in such concerns prudent, reticent, dignified, sensitive on the point of honour; they are rather the faults of a rich middle class,—testy, absolute, ill-acquainted with foreign matters, a little ignoble, very dull to perceive when it is making itself ridiculous.

I know the answer one gets at home when one says that England is not very highly considered just now on the Continent. There is first of all the envy to account for it,—that of course; and then our clear intelligence is making a radical change in our way of dealing with the Continent; the old, bad, aristocratical policy of incessantly intermeddling with the affairs of the Continent,—this it is getting rid of; it is leaving the miserable foreigners to themselves, to their wars, despotisms, bureaucracy, and hatred of free, prosperous England. A few inconveniences may arise before the transition from our old policy to our new is fairly accomplished, and we quite leave off the habit of meddling where our own interests are not at stake. We may be exposed to a little mortification in the passage, but our clear intelligence will discern any occasion where our interests are really at stake. Then we shall come forward and prove ourselves as strong as ever; and the foreigners, in spite of their envy, know it. But what strikes me so much in all which these foreigners say is, that it is just this clear intelligence of ours that they appear at the present moment to hold cheap. Englishmen are often heard complaining of the little gratitude foreign nations show them for their sympathy, their good-will. The reason is, that the foreigners think that an Englishman's good-will to a foreign cause, or dislike to it, is never grounded in a perception of its real merits and bearings, but in some chance circumstance. They say the Englishman never, in these cases, really comprehends the situation, and so they can never feel him to be in living sympathy with them. I have got into much trouble for calling my countrymen Philistines, and all through these remarks I am determined never to use that word; but I wonder if there can be anything offensive in calling one's countryman a young man from the country. I hope not; and if not, I should say, for the benefit of those who have seen Mr. John Parry's amusing entertainment, that England and Englishmen, holding forth on some great crisis in a foreign country,—Poland, say, or Italy,—are apt to have on foreigners very much the effect of the young man from the country who talks to the nursemaid after she has upset the perambulator. There is a terrible crisis, and the discourse of the young man from the country, excellent in itself, is felt not to touch the crisis vitally. Nevertheless, on he goes; the perambulator lies a wreck, the child screams, the nursemaid wrings her hands, the old gentleman storms, the policeman gesticulates, the crowd thickens; still, that astonishing young man talks on, serenely unconscious that he is not at the centre of the situation.

Happening to be much thrown with certain foreigners who criticised England in this sort of way, I used often to think what a short and ready way one of our hard-hitting English newspapers would take with these scorners, if they fell into its hands. But being myself a mere seeker for truth, with nothing trenchant or authoritative about me, I could do no more than look shocked and begin to ask questions. 'What!' I said, 'you hold the England of to-day cheap, and declare that we do not comprehend the situation; yet you rate the England of 1815 so high, and call our fathers and grandfathers the foremost people in Europe. Did they comprehend the situation better than we?' 'Yes,' replied my foreign friends, 'the situation as they had it, a great deal better. Their time was a time for energy, and they succeeded in it, perfectly. Our time is a time for intelligence, and you are not succeeding in it at all.'

Though I could not hear without a shudder this insult to the earnest good sense which, as the *Morning Star* says, may be fairly set down as the general characteristic of England and Englishmen everywhere, yet I pricked up my ears when my companions talked of energy, and England's success in a time for energy, because I have always had a notion myself that energy,—energy with honesty,—is England's great force; a greater force to her, even, than her talent for penetrating through sophisms and ignoring commonplaces; so I begged my acquaintances to explain a little more fully to me what they meant. 'Nothing can be clearer,' they answered. 'Your *Times* was telling you the other day, with the enlightenment it so often shows at present, that instead of being proud of Waterloo and the great war which was closed by it, it really seemed as if you ought rather to feel embarrassed at the recollection of them, since the policy for which they were fought is grown obsolete; the world has taken a turn which was not Lord Castlereagh's, and to look back on the great Tory war is to look back upon an endless account of blood and treasure wasted. Now, that is not so at all. What France had in her head, from the Convention, "faithful to the principles of the sovereignty of the people, which will not permit them to acknowledge anywhere the institutions militating against it," to Napoleon, with his "immense projects for assuring to France the empire of the world,"—what she had in her head, along with many better and sounder notions destined to a happier fortune, was *supremacy*. She had always a vision of a sort of federation of the States of Europe under the primacy of France. Now to this the world, whose progress no doubt lies in the direction of more concert and common purpose among nations, but these nations free, self-impelled, and living each its own life, was not moving. Whoever knocks to pieces a scheme of this sort does the world a service. In antiquity, Roman empire had a scheme of this sort, and much more. The barbarians knocked it to pieces;—honour to the barbarians. In the middle ages Frederick the Second had a scheme of this sort. The Papacy knocked it to pieces;—honour to the Papacy. In our own century, France had a scheme of this sort. Your fathers knocked it to pieces;—honour to your fathers. They were just the people to do it. They had a vigorous lower class, a vigorous middle class, and a vigorous aristocracy. The lower class worked and fought, the middle class found the money, and the aristocracy wielded the whole. This aristocracy was high-spirited, reticent, firm, despising frothy declamation. It had all the qualities useful for its task and time; Lord Grenville's words, as early as 1793: "England will never consent that France shall arrogate the power of annulling at her pleasure, and under the pretence of a pretended natural right, the political system of Europe,"—these few words, with their lofty strength, contain, as one may say, the prophecy of future success; you hear the very voice of an aristocracy standing on sure ground, and with the stars in its favour. Well, you succeeded, and in 1815, after Waterloo, you were the first power in Europe. "These people have a secret," we all said; "they have discerned the way the world was going, and therefore they have prevailed; while, on the other hand, the 'stars in their courses fought against Sisera.'" We held you in the greatest respect; we tried to copy your constitutional government; we read your writers. "After the peace," says George Sand, "the literature of Great Britain crossed the straits, and came to reign amongst us." It reigned in Byron and Scott, voices of the great aristocratical spirit which had just' won the victory:

Scott expressing its robust, genial conservatism, holding by a thousand roots to the past; Byron its defiant force and indomitable pride.

'We believed in you for a good while; but gradually it began to dawn upon us that the era for which you had had the secret was over, and that a new era, for which you had not the secret, was beginning. The work of the old era was to prevent the formation of a second Roman empire, and to maintain a store of free, rich, various national lives for the future to work with and bring to harmony. This was a work of force, of energy: it was a work for an aristocratical power, since, as you yourself are always saying, aristocracies, poor in ideas, are rich in energy. You were a great aristocratical power, and did it. But then came an era with another work, a work of which it is the great glory of the French Revolution (pardon us for saying so, we know it makes some of your countrymen angry to hear it,) passionately to have embraced the idea: the work of making human life, hampered by a past which it has outgrown, natural and rational. This is a work of intelligence, and in intelligence an aristocratic power, as you know, does not so much shine. Accordingly, since the world has been steadily moving this way, you seem to have lost your secret, and we are gradually ceasing to believe in you. You will say, perhaps, that England is no longer an aristocratical power, but a middle-class power, wielded by an industrial middle class, as the England of your fathers was wielded by a territorial aristocracy. This may be so; and indeed, as the style, carriage, and policy of England have of late years been by no means those of an aristocratical power, it probably is so. But whatever class dictates it, your course, allow us to say, has not of late years been intelligent; has not, at any rate, been successful. And depend upon it, a nation who has the secret of her era, who discerns which way the world is going, is successful, keeps rising. Can you yourselves, with all your powers of self-satisfaction, suppose that the Crimean war raised you, or that your Indian mutiny raised you, or that your attitude in the Italian war raised you, as your performances at the beginning of the century raised you? Surely you cannot. You held your own, if you will; you showed tenacity; you saved yourselves from disaster; but you did not raise yourselves, did not advance one jot. Can you, on the other hand, suppose that your attitude in the Danish business, in the American business, has not lowered you? You are losing the instinct which tells people how the world is going; you are beginning to make mistakes; you are falling out of the front rank. The era of aristocracies is over; nations must now stand or fall by the intelligence of their middle class and their people. The people with you is still an embryo; no one can yet quite say what it will come to. You lean, therefore, with your whole weight upon the intelligence of your middle class. And intelligence, in the true sense of the word, your middle class has absolutely none.'

I was aghast. I thought of this great class, every morning and evening extolled for its clear, manly intelligence by a hundred vigorous and influential writers; and though the fine enthusiasm of these writers had always seemed to me to be carrying them a little too far, and I had even been guilty of the indecency of now and then calling my countrymen Philistines, these foreign critics struck me as passing all bounds, and quite out-Heroding Herod. Fortunately I had just received from England a copy of Mr. Lowe's powerful and much-admired speech against Reform. I took it out of my pocket. 'Now,' said I to my envious, carping foreigners, 'just listen to me. You say that the early years of this century were a time for energy, and we did well in them; you say that the last thirty or forty years have been a time for intelligence, and we have done ill in them. Mr. Lowe shall answer you. Here is his reading of our last thirty or forty years' history, as made by our middle-class Parliament, as he calls it; by a Parliament, therefore, filled by the mind and will of this great class whose rule you disparage. Mr. Lowe says: "The seven Houses of Commons that have sate since the Reform Bill have performed exploits unrivalled, not merely in the six centuries during which Parliament has existed, but in the whole history of representative assemblies." He says: "Look at the noble work, the heroic work which the House of Commons has performed within these thirty-five years. It has gone through and revised every institution of the country; it has scanned our trade, our colonies, our laws, and our municipal institutions; everything that was complained of, everything that had grown distasteful, has been touched with success and moderation by the amending hand. And to such a point have these amendments been carried, that when gentlemen come to argue this question, and do all in their power to get up a practical grievance, they fail in suggesting even one." There is what Mr. Lowe says. You see we have nothing left to desire, absolutely nothing. As Mr. Lowe himself goes on: "With all this continued peace, contentment, happiness, and prosperity,—England in its present state of development and civilisation,—the mighty fabric of English prosperity,—what can we want more?" Evidently nothing! therefore to propose "for England to make a step in the direction of democracy is the strangest and wildest proposition ever broached by man." People talk of America. "In America the working classes are the masters; does anybody doubt that?" And compare, Mr. Lowe means, England, as the middle class is making her, with America, as the working classes are making her. How entirely must the comparison turn to the advantage of the English middle class! Then, finally, as to the figure we cut in the eyes of the world, our grandeur and our future, here is a crowning sentence, worthy of Lord Macaulay himself, whose style Mr. Lowe enthusiastically admires: "*The destiny of England is in the great heart of England!*"'

Mr. Bright had not then made his famous speech about the misdeeds of the Tories, but, if he had, I should certainly have added that our middle class, by these unrivalled exploits of theirs, had not only raised their country to an unprecedented height of greatness, but had also saved our foolish and obstructive aristocracy from being emptied into the Thames.

As it was, however, what I had urged, or rather what I had borrowed from Mr. Lowe, seemed to me exceedingly forcible, and I looked anxiously for its effect on my hearers. They did not appear so much disconcerted as I had hoped. 'Undoubtedly,' they said, 'the coming of your middle class to power was a natural salutary event, to be blessed, not anathematised. Aristocracies cannot deal with a time for intelligence; their sense is for facts, not ideas. The world of ideas is the possible, the future; the world of aristocracies is the established, the past, which has made their fortune, and which they hope to prolong. No doubt, too, your middle class found a great deal of commercial and social business waiting to be done, which your aristocratic governments had left undone, and had no talents for doing. Their talents were for other times and tasks; for curbing the power of the Crown when other classes were too inconsiderable to do it; for managing (if one compares them with other aristocracies) their affairs and their dependants with vigour, prudence, and moderation, during the feudal and patriarchal stage of society; for wielding the force of their country against foreign powers with energy, firmness, and dignity. But then came the modern spirit, the modern time; the notion, as we say, of making human life more natural and rational,—or, as your philosophers say, of getting the greatest happiness for the greatest number. Have you succeeded, are you succeeding, in this hour of the many, as your aristocracy succeeded in the hour of the few? You say you are: you point to "the noble work, the heroic work which the House of Commons has performed within these last thirty-five years; everything that was complained of, everything that had grown distasteful, has been touched with success and moderation by the amending hand." Allow us to set clap-trap on one side; we are not at one of your public meetings. What is the modern problem? to make human life, the life of society, all through, more natural and rational; to have the greatest possible number of one's nation happy. Here is the standard by which we are to try ourselves and one another now, as national grandeur, in the old regal and aristocratical conception of it, was the standard formerly. Every nation must have wished to be England, in 1815, tried by the old standard: must we all wish to be England, in 1865, tried by the new standard? Your aristocracy, you say, is as splendid, as fortunate, as enviable as ever: very likely; but all the world cannot be aristocracy. What do you make of the mass of your society, of its vast middle and lower portion? Are we to envy you your common people; is our common people to wish to change places with yours; are we to say that you, more than we, have the modern secret here? Without insisting too much on the stories of misery and degradation which are perpetually reaching us, we will say that no one can mix with a great crowd in your country, no one can walk with his eyes and ears open through the poor quarters of your large towns, and not feel that your common people, as it meets one's eyes, is at present more raw, to say the very least, less enviable-looking, further removed from civilised and humane life, than the common people almost anywhere. Well, then, you are not a success, according to the modern standard, with your common people. Are you a success with your middle class? They have the power now; what have they made of themselves? what sort of a life is theirs? A life more natural, more rational, fuller of happiness, more enviable, therefore, than the life of the middle classes on the Continent? Yes, you will say, because the English middle class is the most industrious and the richest. But it is just here that you go a great deal too fast, and so deceive yourselves. What brings about, or rather tends to bring about, a natural, rational life, satisfying the modern spirit? This: the growth of a love of industry, trade, and wealth; the growth of a love of the things of the mind; and the growth of a love of beautiful things. There are body, intelligence, and soul all taken care of. Of these three factors of modern life, your middle class has no notion of any but one, the first. Their love of industry, trade, and wealth, is certainly prodigious; and their example has done us a great deal of good; we, too, are beginning to get this love, and we wanted it. But what notion have they of anything else? Do but look at them, look at their lives. Some of us know your middle class very well; a great deal better than your own upper class in general knows them. Your middle class is educated, to begin with, in the worst schools of your country, and our middle class is educated in the best of ours. What becomes of them after that? The fineness and capacity of a man's spirit is shown by his enjoyments; your middle class has an enjoyment in its business, we admit, and gets on well in business, and makes money; but beyond that? Drugged with business, your middle class seems to have its sense blunted for any stimulus besides, except religion; it has a religion, narrow, unintelligent, repulsive. All sincere religion does something for the spirit, raises a man out of the bondage of his merely bestial part, and saves him; but the religion of your middle class is the very lowest form of intelligential life which one can imagine as saving. What other enjoyments have they? The newspapers, a sort of eating and drinking which are not to our taste, a literature of books almost entirely religious or semi-religious, books utterly unreadable by an educated class anywhere, but which your middle class consumes, they say, by the hundred thousand; and in their evenings, for a great treat, a lecture on teetotalism or nunneries. Can any life be imagined more hideous, more dismal, more unenviable? Compare it with the life of our middle class as you have seen it on the Rhine this summer, or at Lausanne, or Zurich. The world of enjoyment, so liberalising and civilising, belongs to the middle classes there, as well as the world of business; the whole world is theirs, they possess life; in England the highest class seems to have the monopoly of the world of enjoyment, the middle class enjoys itself, as your Shakspeare would say, in hugger-mugger, and possesses life only by reading in the newspapers, which it does devoutly, the doings of great people. Well then, we do not at all want to be as your middle class; we want to learn from it to do business and to get rich, and this we are learning a great deal faster than you think; but we do not, like your middle class, fix our consummation here: we have a notion of a whole world besides, not dreamed of in your middle class's philosophy; so they, too, like your common people, seem to us no success. They may be the masters of the modern time with you, but they are not solving its problem. They cannot see the way the world is going, and the future does not belong to them. Talk of the present state of development and civilisation of England, meaning England as they represent it to us! Why, the capital, pressing danger of England, is the barbarism of her middle class; the civilisation of her middle class is England's capital, pressing want.'

'Well, but,' said I, still catching at Mr. Lowe's powerful help, 'the Parliament of this class has performed exploits unrivalled not merely in the six centuries during which Parliament has existed, but in the whole history of representative assemblies. The exploits are there; all the reforms we have made in the last five-and-thirty years.'

'Let us distinguish,' replied the envious foreigners, 'let us distinguish. We named three powers,—did we not?—which go to spread that rational humane life which is the aim of modern society: the love of wealth, the love of intelligence, the love of beauty. Your middle class, we agreed, has the first; its commercial legislation, accordingly, has been very good, and in advance of that of foreign countries. Not that free-trade was really brought about by your middle class: it was brought about, as important reforms always are, by two or three great men. However, let your middle class, which had the sense to accept free-trade, have the credit of it. But this only brings us a certain way. The legislation of your middle class in all that goes to give human life more intelligence and beauty, is no better than was to be expected from its own want of both. It is nothing to say that its legislation in these respects is an improvement upon what you had before; that is not the question; you are holding up its achievements as absolutely admirable, as unrivalled, as a model to us. You may have done,—for you,—much for religious toleration, social improvement, public instruction, municipal reform, law reform; but the French Revolution and its consequences have done, upon the Continent, a great deal more. Such a spectacle as your Irish Church Establishment[1] you cannot find in France or Germany. Your Irish land-question you hardly dare to face,[2] Stein settled as threatening a land-question in Prussia. Of the schools for your middle class we have already spoken; while these schools are what they are, while the schools for your poor are maintained in the expensive, unjust, irrational way they are, England is full of endowments and foundations, capable by themselves, if properly applied, of putting your public education on a much better footing. In France and Germany all similar funds are thus employed, having been brought under public responsible management; in England they are left to private irresponsible management, and are, in nine cases out of ten, wasted. You talk of municipal reform; and cities and the manner of life in them have, for the modern business of promoting a more rational and humane life in the great body of the community, incalculable importance. Do you suppose we should tolerate in France, Germany, Switzerland, Italy, your London corporation and London vestries, and London as they make it? In your provincial towns you do better; but even there, do the municipalities show a tenth part either of the intelligence or the care for the ends, as we have laid them down, of

[1] It is gone, thanks to Anti-State-Church-ism!—Ed.

[2] We have faced it!—Ed.

modern society, that our municipalities show? Your middle-class man thinks it the highest pitch of development and civilisation when his letters are carried twelve times a day from Islington to Camberwell, and from Camberwell to Islington, and if railway-trains run to and fro between them every quarter of an hour. He thinks it is nothing that the trains only carry him from an illiberal, dismal life at Islington to an illiberal, dismal life at Camberwell; and the letters only tell him that such is the life there. A Swiss burgher takes heaven knows how many hours to go from Berne to Geneva, and his trains are very few; this is an extreme on the other side; but compare the life the Swiss burgher finds or leaves at Berne or Geneva with the life of the middle class in your English towns. Or else you think to cover everything by saying: "We are free! we are free! Our newspapers can say what they like!" Freedom, like Industry, is a very good horse to ride;—but to ride somewhere. You seem to think that you have only got to get on the back of your horse Freedom, or your horse Industry, and to ride away as hard as you can, to be sure of coming to the right destination. If your newspapers can say what they like, you think you are sure of being well advised. That comes of your inaptitude for ideas, and aptitude for clap-trap; you can never see the two sides of a question; never perceive that every human state of things, even a good one, has its inconveniences. We can see the conveniences of your state well enough, and the inconveniences of ours; of newspapers not free, and prefects over-busy; and there are plenty of us who proclaim them. You eagerly repeat after us all we say that redounds to your own honour and glory; but you never follow our example yourselves. You are full of acuteness to perceive the ill influence of our prefects on us; but if any one says to you, in your turn: "The English system of a great landed aristocracy [1] keeps your lower class a lower class for ever, and materialises and vulgarises your whole middle class,"—you stare vacantly at the speaker, you cannot even take in his ideas; you can only blurt forth, in reply, some clap-trap or other about a "system of such tried and tested efficiency as no other country was ever happy enough to possess since the world was a world."'

I have observed in my travels, that most young gentlemen of our highest class go through Europe, from Calais

[1] What a contrast between this Jacobinism and the noble sentiments of Barrow: 'Men will never be heartily loyal and submissive to authority till they become really good; nor will they ever be very good, till they see their leaders such.' I remember once quoting this passage to Arminius at the time when we were all full of the Mordaunt trial. 'Yes,' remarked Arminius, in his thoughtful manner, 'that is what makes your Lord Coles so inexpressibly precious!' But was this an answer? I say not.—Ed.

to Constantinople, with one sentence on their lips, and one idea in their minds, which suffices, apparently, to explain all that they see to them: *Foreigners don't wash.* No doubt, thought I to myself, my friends have fallen in with some distinguished young Britons of this sort, and had their feelings wounded by them; hence their rancour against our aristocracy. And as to our middle class, foreigners have no notion how much this class, with us, contains; how many shades and gradations in it there are, and how little what is said of one part of it will apply to another. Something of this sort I could not help urging aloud. 'You do not know,' I said, 'that there is broken off, as one may say, from the top of our middle class, a large fragment, which receives the best education the country can give, the same education as our aristocracy; which is perfectly intelligent and which enjoys life perfectly. These men do the main part of our intellectual work, write all our best newspapers; and cleverer people, I assure you, are nowhere to be found.'

'Clever enough,' was the answer, 'but they show not much intelligence, in the true sense of the word,—not much intelligence of the way the world is going. Whether it is that they must try to hit your current public opinion, which is not intelligent; whether it is that, having been, as you say, brought up with your aristocracy, they have been too much influenced by it, have taken, half insensibly, an aristocracy's material standard, and do not believe in ideas; certain it is that their intelligence has no ardour, no plan, leads them nowhere; it is ineffectual. Your intellect is at this moment, to an almost unexampled degree, without influence on the intellect of Europe.'

While this was being said, I noticed an Italian,[1] who was one of our party, fumbling with his pocket-book, from whence he presently produced a number of grey newspaper slips, which I could see were English. 'Now just listen to me for a moment,' he cried, 'and I will show you what makes us say, on the Continent, that you English have no sense for logic, for ideas, and that your praise and blame, having no substantial foundation, are worth very little. You remember the famous French pamphlet before our war began in 1859: *Napoleon the Third and Italy.* The pamphlet appealed, in the French way, to reason and first principles; the upshot of it was this: "The treaties which bind governments would be invariable only if the world was immovable. A power which should intrench itself behind treaties in order to resist modifications demanded by general feeling would have doubtless on her side an acquired right, but she would have against her moral right and universal conscience." You English, on

[1] Little Pompeo Pococurante. Almost all the rest is Arminius.

the other hand, took your stand on things as they were: "If treaties are made," said your *Times*, "they must be respected. Tear one, and all are waste paper." Very well; this is a policy, at any rate, an aristocratical policy; much may be said for it. The *Times* was full of contempt for the French pamphlet, an essay, as it called it, "conveying the dreams of an agitator expressed in the language of an academician." It said: "No one accustomed to the pithy comments with which liberty notices passing history, can read such a production without complacency that he does not live in the country which produces it. To see the heavy apparatus of an essay brought out to solve a question on which men have corresponded and talked and speculated in the funds, and acted in the most practical manner possible for a month past, is as strange as if we beheld some spectral review," and so on. Still very well; there is the strong practical man despising theories and reveries. "The sentiment of race is just now threatening to be exceedingly troublesome. It is to a considerable extent in our days a literary revival." That is all to the same effect. Then came a hitch in our affairs, and fortune seemed as if she was going to give, as she often does give, the anti-theorists a triumph. "The Italian plot," cried the *Times*, "has failed. The Emperor and his familiars knew not the moral strength which is still left in the enlightened communities of Europe. To the unanimous and indignant reprobation of English opinion is due the failure of the imperial plots. While silence and fear reign everywhere abroad, the eyes and ears of the Continent are turned continually to these Islands. English opinion has been erected into a kind of Areopagus." Our business went forward again, and your English opinion grew very stern indeed. "Sardinia," said the *Times*, "is told very plainly that she has deserted the course by which alone she could hope either to be happy or great, and abandoned herself to the guidance of fatal delusions, which are luring her on to destruction. By cultivating the arts of peace she would have been solving, in the only possible way, the difficult problem of Italian independence. She has been taught by France to look instead to the acquisition of fresh territory by war and conquest. She has now been told with perfect truth by the warning voice of the British Parliament that she has not a moment to lose in retracing her steps, if indeed her penitence be not too late." Well, to make a long story short, we did not retrace our steps; we went on, as you know; we succeeded; and now let us make a jump from the spring to the autumn. Here is your unanimous English opinion, here is your Areopagus, here is your *Times*, in October: "It is very irregular (Sardinia's course), it is contrary to all diplomatic forms.

Francis the Second can show a thousand texts of international law against it. Yes; but there are extremities beyond all law, and there are laws which existed before even society was formed. There are laws which are implanted in our nature, and which form part of the human mind," and so on. Why, here you have entirely boxed the compass and come round from the aristocratical programme to the programme of the French pamphlet, "the dreams of an agitator in the language of an academician!" And you approved not only our present but our past, and kindly took off your ban of reprobation issued in February. "How great a change has been effected by the wisely courageous policy of Sardinia! The firmness and boldness which have raised Italy from degradation form the enduring character of a ten years' policy. King Victor Emmanuel and his sagacious counsellor have achieved success by remembering that fortune favours the bold." There you may see why the mind of France influences the Continent so much and the mind of England so little. France has intelligence enough to perceive the ideas that are moving, or are likely to move, the world; she believes in them, sticks to them, and shapes her course to suit them. You neither perceive them nor believe in them, but you play with them like counters, taking them up and laying them down at random, and following really some turn of your imagination, some gust of liking or disliking. When I heard some of your countrymen complaining of Italy and her ingratitude for English sympathy, I made, to explain it, the collection of those extracts and of a good many more. They are all at your service; I have some here from the *Saturday Review*, which you will find exactly follow suit with those from the *Times*.' 'No, thank you,' I answered. 'The *Times* is enough. My relations with the *Saturday Review* are rather tight-stretched, as you say here, already; make me a party to none of your quarrels with them.'

After this my original tormentor[1] once more took up his parable. 'You see now what I meant,' he said, 'by saying that you did better in the old time, in the day of aristocracies. An aristocracy has no ideas, but it has a policy,—to resist change. In this policy it believes, it sticks to it; when it is beaten in it, it holds its tongue. This is respectable, at any rate. But your great middle class, as you call it, your present governing power, having no policy, except that of doing a roaring trade, does not know what to be at in great affairs,—blows hot and cold by turns,—makes itself ridiculous, in short. It was a good aristocratical policy to have helped Austria in the Italian war; it was a good aristocratical policy to have helped the

[1] Arminius, of course.

South in the American war. The days of aristocratical policy are over for you; with your new middle-class public opinion you cut, in Italy, the figure our friend here has just shown you; in America you scold right and left, you get up a monster-memorial to deprecate the further effusion of blood; you lament over the abridgment of civil liberty by people engaged in a struggle for life and death, and meaning to win; and when they turn a deaf ear to you and win, you say, "Oh, now let us be one great united Anglo-Saxon family and astonish the world!" This is just of a piece with your threatening Germany with the Emperor of the French. Do you not see that all these blunders dispose the Americans, who are very shrewd, and who have been succeeding as steadily as you have been failing, to answer: "We have got the lead, no thanks to you, and we mean to astonish the world without you"? Unless you change, unless your middle class grows more intelligent, you will tell upon the world less and less, and end by being a second Holland. We do not hold you cheap for saying you will wash your hands of all concerns but your own, that you do not care a rush for influence in Europe; though this sentence of your Lord Bolingbroke is true: "The opinion of mankind, which is fame after death, is superior strength and power in life." We hold you cheap because you show so few signs, except in the one department of industry, of understanding your time and its tendencies, and of exhibiting a modern life which shall be a signal success. And the reaction is the stronger, because, after 1815, we believed in you as now-a-days we are coming to believe in America. You had won the last game, and we thought you had your hand full of trumps, and were going to win the next. Now the game has begun to be played, and we have an inkling of what your cards are; we shrewdly suspect you have scarcely any trumps at all.'

I am no arguer, as is well known, 'and every puny whipster gets my sword.'[1] So, instead of making bad worse by a lame answer, I held my tongue, consoling myself with the thought that these foreigners get from us, at any rate, plenty of Rolands for any stray Oliver they may have the luck to give us. I have since meditated a good deal on what was then said, but I cannot profess to be yet quite clear about it. However, all due deductions made for envy, exaggeration, and injustice, enough stuck by me of these remarks on our logic, criticism, and love of intelligence, to determine me to go on trying (taking care, of course, to steer clear of indecency) to keep my mind fixed on these, instead of singing hosannahs

[1] And this is why it was peculiarly unlucky for me to be thrown so much with Arminius, who loved arguing.—ED.

to our actual state of development and civilisation. The old recipe, to think a little more and bustle a little less, seemed to me still the best recipe to follow. So I take comfort when I find the *Guardian* reproaching me with having no influence; for I know what influence means,—a party, practical proposals, action; and I say to myself: 'Even suppose I could get some followers, and assemble them, brimming with affectionate enthusiasm, in a committee-room at some inn; what on earth should I say to them? what resolutions could I propose? I could only propose the old Socratic commonplace, *Know thyself*; and how black they would all look at that!' No; to inquire, perhaps too curiously, what that present state of English development and civilisation is, which according to Mr. Lowe is so perfect that to give votes to the working class is stark madness; and, on the other hand, to be less sanguine about the divine and saving effect of a vote on its possessor than my friends in the committee-room at the 'Spotted Dog,'—that is my inevitable portion. To bring things under the light of one's intelligence, to see how they look there, to accustom oneself simply to regard the Marylebone Vestry, or the Educational Home, or the Irish Church Establishment, or our railway management, or our Divorce Court, or our gin-palaces open on Sunday and the Crystal Palace shut, as absurdities,—that is, I am sure, invaluable exercise for us just at present. Let all persist in it who can, and steadily set their desires on introducing, with time, a little more soul and spirit into the too, too solid flesh of English society.

I have a friend who is very sanguine, in spite of the dismal croakings of these foreigners, about the turn things are even now taking amongst us. 'Mean and ignoble as our middle class looks,' he says, 'it has this capital virtue, it has seriousness. With frivolity, cultured or uncultured, you can do nothing; but with seriousness there is always hope. Then, too, the present bent of the world towards amusing itself, so perilous to the highest class, is curative and good for our middle class. A piano in a Quaker's drawing-room is a step for him to more humane life; nay, perhaps, even the penny gaff of the poor East-Londoner is a step for him to more humane life; it is,—what example shall we choose? it is *Strathmore*, let us say,—it is the one-pound-eleven-and-sixpenny gaff of the young gentlemen of the clubs and the young ladies of Belgravia, that is for them but a step in the primrose path to the everlasting bonfire. Besides, say what you like of the idealessness of aristocracies, the vulgarity of our middle class, the immaturity of our lower, and the poor chance which a happy type of modern life has between them, consider this: Of all that makes life liberal and humane,—of light, of ideas, of culture,—every man in every class of society who has a dash of genius in him is the born friend. By his bringing up, by his habits, by his interest, he may be their enemy; by the primitive, unalterable complexion of his nature, he is their friend. Therefore, the movement of the modern spirit will be more and more felt among us, it will spread, it will prevail. Nay,' this enthusiast often continues, getting excited as he goes on, 'the *Times* itself, which so stirs some people's indignation,—what is the *Times* but a gigantic Sancho Panza, to borrow a phrase of your friend Heine;—a gigantic Sancho Panza, following by an attraction he cannot resist that poor, mad, scorned, suffering, sublime enthusiast, the modern spirit; following it, indeed, with constant grumbling, expostulation, and opposition, with airs of protection, of compassionate superiority, with an incessant byplay of nods, shrugs, and winks addressed to the spectators; following it, in short, with all the incurable recalcitrancy of a lower nature, but still following it?' When my friend talks thus, I always shake my head, and say that this sounds very like the transcendentalism which has already brought me into so many scrapes.

I have another friend again (and I am grown so cowed by all the rebuke my original speculations have drawn upon me that I find myself more and more filling the part of a mere listener), who calls himself Anglo-Saxon rather than English,[1] and this is what he says: 'We are a small country,' he says, 'and our middle class has, as you say, not much gift for anything but making money. Our freedom and wealth have given us a great start, our capital will give us for a long time an advantage; but as other countries grow better-governed and richer, we must necessarily sink to the position to which our size, and our want of any eminent gift for telling upon the world spiritually, doom us. But look at America; it is the same race; whether we are first or they; Anglo-Saxonism triumphs. You used to say that they had all the Philistinism of the English middle class from which they spring, and a great many faults of their own besides. But you noticed, too, that, blindly as they seemed following in general the star of their god Buncombe, they showed, at the same time, a feeling for ideas, a vivacity and play of mind, which our middle class has not, and which comes to the Americans, probably, from their democratic life, with its ardent hope, its forward stride, its gaze fixed on the future. Well, since these great events have lately come to purge and form them, how is this intelligence of theirs developing itself? Now they are manifesting a quick sense to see how the

[1] *Not* the talented author of 'Greater Britain,' though the reader might be inclined to suppose so.—ED.

world is really going, and a sure faith, indispensable to all nations that are to be great, that greatness is only to be reached by going that way and no other? And then, if you talk of culture, look at the culture their middle, and even their working class is getting, as compared with the culture ours are getting. The trash which circulates by the hundred thousand among our middle class has no readers in America; our rubbish is for home-consumption; all our best books, books which are read here only by the small educated class, are in America the books of the great reading public. So over there they will advance spiritually as well as materially; and if our race at last flowers to modern life there, and not here, does it so much matter?' So says my friend, who is, as I premised, a devotee of Anglo-Saxonism; I, who share his pious frenzy but imperfectly, do not feel quite satisfied with these plans of vicarious greatness, and have a longing for this old and great country of ours to be always great in herself, not only in her progeny. So I keep looking at her, and thinking of her; and as often as I consider how history is a series of waves, coming gradually to a head and then breaking, and that, as the successive waves come up, one nation is seen at the top of this wave, and then another of the next, I ask myself, counting all the waves which have come up with England at the top of them: When the great wave which is now mounting has come up, will she be at the top of it? *Illa nihil, nec me quærentem vana moratur!*—

> Yes, we arraign her; but she,
> The weary Titan, with deaf
> Ears, and labour-dimm'd eyes,
> Regarding neither to right
> Nor left, goes passively by,
> Staggering on to her goal;
> Bearing, on shoulders immense,
> Atlantéan, the load,
> Wellnigh not to be borne,
> Of the too vast orb of her fate

(A FRENCHMAN signing himself 'Horace,'—not one of our own set, but a person full of intellect,—wrote to the Editor of the *Pall Mall Gazette* a sort of electioneering letter from Paris in answer to the foregoing essay, saying what blessings our liberty and publicity were, and how miserable the French middle class was without them. I cannot do better than conclude with the answer I made to him, from which it will appear, I hope, how courteous was always my moderation when I was left to myself, and had not Arminius at my elbow to make me say what he chose. I should premise that 'My Countrymen' had been received with such a storm of obloquy, that for several months after its appearance I was in hiding;—not, indeed, leaving Grub Street, but changing my lodgings there repeatedly.)—ED.

A Courteous Explanation.

SIR,— *Grub Street, March* 19, 1866.

ALTHOUGH I certainly am rather pained to find myself, after my long and arduous labours for the deliverance from Philistinism of this nation in general, and the civilisation and embellishment of our great middle class in particular, an object of aversion and mistrust to my countrymen, when I expected nothing from them but gratitude and love, still I have learnt to try and wrap myself on these occasions in my own virtue, knowing very well that the benefactors of mankind are seldom popular, and that your public favourite is generally some Barabbas. Meanwhile, for posterity's sake, I keep out of harm's way as much as I can; but as I sit shivering in my garret, listening nervously to the voices of indignant Philistines asking the way to Grub Street, a friend brings me the *Pall Mall Gazette* with 'Horace's' two letters. Perhaps it would be my best way to keep perfectly still, and not to give any sign of life to my enemies; but such is my inveterate weakness (dear enough it has cost me, this weakness !) for the amiable nation to which 'Horace' belongs, that I cannot find it in my heart to leave his letters without a word of acknowledgment. I write with a bit of coal on the lining of my hat, and in much perturbation of mind besides; so 'Horace' will kindly excuse faults in my style, which indeed, as he has observed, even when I am at my best, is far from correct. But what is one to do? So few people know what it is to be born artless.

It is very kind of 'Horace,' and just like his generous nation, to come forward when he sees I am in trouble, to confirm what he thinks I said; only I did not say it, but the foreigners. 'Horace' says that with us mediocrity does make itself heard more loudly and more frequently than the thoughtful part of the nation, through the press and even in Parliament; he says that he is inclined to think the middle classes in Germany and Switzerland enjoy life more than the same classes in England; he says he is quite of opinion that the conduct of England in the affair of the Duchies lowered her considerably in the eyes of Europe, nor did she gain honour by the Crimean war, or by her attitude in Italian affairs. He adds, indeed, that it is probable some fifty years hence certain episodes of the Indian mutiny, and the heroism and charity displayed during the cotton famine, will be accepted as a set-off for many shortcomings; and I am sure I devoutly hope they may; but my foreign friends were only talking of the present.

It was the life of the middle class in Switzerland and Germany that my foreign friends said was more enjoyable than the life of the corresponding class in England, and 'Horace' declares my foreign friends were right. But he goes on to draw a frightful picture of the middle class in his own country, France. This is what I so admire in these continental writers, and it is just what my foreign friends claimed for them: 'We foreigners can see our own deficiencies well enough, and are not backward in proclaiming them; you English can see and say nothing but what redounds to your own honour and glory.' It makes me blush to think how I winced under what the foreigners said of England, how I longed to be able to answer it, how I rejoiced at hearing from the English press that there was nothing at all in it, when I see the noble frankness with which these foreigners judge themselves. How 'Horace' does give it to his poor countrymen when he thinks they deserve it! So did Monsieur de Tocqueville, so does Monsieur Renan. I lay up the example for my own edification, and I commend it to the editor of the *Morning Star* for his.

I have seen very little of the French middle class which

'Horace' describes, and I daresay what he says of them is all true. But what makes me look at France and the French with such inexhaustible curiosity and indulgence is this,—their faults are not ours, so we are not likely to catch them; their merits are not ours, so we are not likely to become idle and self-sufficient from studying them. It is not that I so envy 'Horace' his Paris as it is;—I no longer dance, nor look well when dressed up as the angel Gabriel, so what should I now do in Paris?—but I find such interest and instruction in considering a city so near London, and yet so unlike it! It is not that I so envy 'Horace' his café-haunting, dominoes-playing *bourgeois*; but when I go through Saint Pancras, I like to compare our vestry-haunting, resolution-passing *bourgeois* with the Frenchman, and to say to myself: 'This, then, is what comes of not frequenting cafés, nor playing dominoes! My countrymen here have got no cafés, and have never learnt dominoes, and see the mischief Satan has found for their idle hands to do!' Still, I do not wish them to be the café-haunting, dominoes-playing Frenchmen, but rather some third thing, neither the Frenchmen nor their present selves.

And this brings me to the one little point of difference (for there is just one) between 'Horace' and me. Everything, as he himself says, depends on a man's point of view. Now, his point of view is French, mine English. He and his friends have, he says, one absorbing desire,—to diffuse in France the knowledge and love of true political liberty. For this purpose they are obliged to point to other countries, and England is, says 'Horace,' their 'great stand-by.' Now, those who speak evil of the English constituencies, of our great middle class, &c. &c., discredit, 'Horace says, English parliamentary government and the power of the press, and tend to damage the great stalking-horse behind which he and his friends are moving to the attack of the French Emperor, and so spoil their game for them.

'Horace' and his friends are evidently Orleanists, and I have always observed that the Orleanists are rather sly. They can put their tongue in their cheek as well as anybody at the expense of my dear country, but she is to be an angel of light as long as it serves their turn. So the *Morning Star* and I are to go on crying, 'We are free! we are free! Our newspapers can say what they like,' whether this cry does us good or no, because true political liberty is the one thing needful for 'Horace' and the French. The *Morning Star*, I must say, does its duty nobly, and 'Horace' ought to be very grateful to it; but because I, thinking only of England, venture to go on a little farther, and to inquire what we do with ourselves when we are free to do just what we like, I give umbrage to 'Horace;' he says I destroy his stalking-horse, and he accuses me of railing at parliamentary government and the power of the press. In short, he and his friends have lost their tails, and want to get them back again ; and unless I talk of nothing but tails, and keep always saying that whoever has a tail is perfect, and whoever has not a tail is not worth twopence, 'Horace' is vexed with me.

To prevent all such misunderstanding for the future, let me say, in the fullest, frankest, most unreserved manner, that I admit the French have lost their tails, and that I pity them for it. I rejoice that the English have kept theirs. I think our 'true political liberty' a beautiful, bushy object, and whoever says I do not think so slanders me. But I do not see the slightest danger of our losing it. Well, then comes the question, whether, to oblige 'Horace' and his friends, I am to talk of nothing but this beautiful tail of ours, and our good fortune in having it. I should not mind doing this if our human economy took in nothing but tails, if we were all tail ; but our economy takes in other things as well,—hearts, for instance, and heads. In hearts we are (except when we find ourselves in India or Jamaica) very well off; but in heads there is always room for improvement. Now, I think it was after witnessing a great constitutional stand by the Saint Pancras Board of Guardians,—no, it was after reading the second or third of the *Daily Telegraph's* funeral orations on Lord

Palmerston,—that it struck me there was a danger of our trading too extensively upon our tails, and, in fact, running to tail altogether. I determined to try and preach up the improvement and decoration of our heads. Our highest class, besides having of course true political liberty,—that regulation tail which every Briton of us is blessed with,—is altogether so beautiful and splendid [1] that for my part I hardly presume to inquire what it has or has not in the way of heads. So I turn to my own class, the middle class, which, not being so beautiful and splendid, does not dazzle my eyes so much. And for this class I want to work out a deliverance from the horrid dilemma in which 'Horace' and others try to fix us;—liberty and Philistinism, or else culture and slavery.

After this candid explanation on our one point of difference (for the rest of his letters I heartily thank him), I trust that 'Horace' will not in future think it his duty, whenever he finds me preaching to my countrymen that with all our political liberty we are still, in many respects, unprofitable servants,—I trust, I say, that whenever he sees this, he will not now think it his duty to administer to me a sharp pinch and exclaim: 'False one, what are you about? what have you done with your tail? begin brandishing it in our tyrant's face again directly!' Let him and

[1] And above all, as Mr. Carlyle says, *polite*.—ED.

the French rather themselves get back their lost tails from their tyrant, who is generally supposed, too, to have had, when he talked of 'crowning the edifice,' this appendage in view.

I do hope, Sir, that the sentiments expressed in this letter may be the means of procuring for your excellent newspaper that free circulation in the French capital which is at present, I am told, denied you; and as my bit of coal is worn to a stump, I sign myself, your humble servant,

MATTHEW ARNOLD.

To

The EDITOR *of the* PALL MALL GAZETTE.